# EXCAVATION

# ARCHAEOLOGIST'S TOOLKIT

SERIES EDITORS: LARRY J. ZIMMERMAN AND WILLIAM GREEN

The Archaeologist's Toolkit is an integrated set of seven volumes designed to teach novice archaeologists and students the basics of doing archaeological fieldwork, analysis, and presentation. Students are led through the process of designing a study, doing survey work, excavating, properly working with artifacts and biological remains, curating their materials, and presenting findings to various audiences. The volumes—written by experienced field archaeologists—are full of practical advice, tips, case studies, and illustrations to help the reader. All of this is done with careful attention to promoting a conservation ethic and an understanding of the legal and practical environment of contemporary American cultural resource laws and regulations. The Toolkit is an essential resource for anyone working in the field and ideal for training archaeology students in classrooms and field schools.

**Volume 1: *Archaeology by Design***
*Stephen L. Black and Kevin Jolly*

**Volume 2: *Archaeological Survey***
*By James M. Collins and Brian Leigh Molyneaux*

**Volume 3: *Excavation***
*By David L. Carmichael, Robert H. Lafferty III, and Brian Leigh Molyneaux*

**Volume 4: *Artifacts***
*By Charles R. Ewen*

**Volume 5: *Archaeobiology***
*By Kristin D. Sobolik*

**Volume 6: *Curating Archaeological Collections:***
   ***From the Field to the Repository***
*By Lynne P. Sullivan and S. Terry Childs*

**Volume 7: *Presenting the Past***
*By Larry J. Zimmerman*

# EXCAVATION

## DAVID L. CARMICHAEL
## ROBERT H. LAFFERTY III
## BRIAN LEIGH MOLYNEAUX

ARCHAEOLOGIST'S TOOLKIT
VOLUME 3

A Division of Rowman & Littlefield Publishers, Inc.
Walnut Creek • Lanham • New York • Oxford

ALTAMIRA PRESS
A division of Rowman & Littlefield Publishers, Inc.
1630 North Main Street, #367
Walnut Creek, CA 94596
www.altamirapress.com

Rowman & Littlefield Publishers, Inc.
A wholly owned subsidiary of The Rowman & Littlefield Publishing Group, Inc.
4501 Forbes Boulevard, Suite 200
Lanham, MD 20706

PO Box 317
Oxford
OX2 9RU, UK

British Library Cataloguing in Publication Information Available

**Library of Congress Cataloging-in-Publication Data**
Carmichael, David L.
    Excavation / David L. Carmichael, Robert H. Lafferty III, and Brian
Leigh Molyneaux.
        p. cm.—(Archaeologist's toolkit ; v. 3)
Includes bibliographical references and index.
    ISBN 0-7591-0399-2 (hardcover : alk. paper)—ISBN 0-7591-0019-5
(pbk. : alk. paper)
    1. Excavations (Archaeology) 2. Archaeology—Field work. I.
Lafferty, Robert H. II. Molyneaux, Brian Leigh. III. Title. IV. Series.

    CC76.C37 2003
    930.1'028'3—dc21

                                                        2003012124

Printed in the United States of America

∞™ The paper used in this publication meets the minimum requirements of
American National Standard for Information Sciences—Permanence of Paper
for Printed Library Materials, ANSI/NISO Z39.48–1992.

 CONTENTS

# SERIES EDITORS' FOREWORD

The Archaeologist's Toolkit is a series of books on how to plan, design, carry out, and use the results of archaeological research. The series contains seven books written by acknowledged experts in their fields. Each book is a self-contained treatment of an important element of modern archaeology. Therefore, each book can stand alone as a reference work for archaeologists in public agencies, private firms, and museums, as well as a textbook and guidebook for classrooms and field settings. The books function even better as a set, because they are integrated through cross-references and complementary subject matter.

Archaeology is a rapidly growing field, one that is no longer the exclusive province of academia. Today, archaeology is a part of daily life in both the public and private sectors. Thousands of archaeologists apply their knowledge and skills every day to understand the human past. Recent explosive growth in archaeology has heightened the need for clear and succinct guidance on professional practice. Therefore, this series supplies ready reference to the latest information on methods and techniques—the tools of the trade that serve as handy guides for longtime practitioners and essential resources for archaeologists in training.

Archaeologists help solve modern problems: They find, assess, recover, preserve, and interpret the evidence of the human past in light of public interest and in the face of multiple land use and development interests. Most of North American archaeology is devoted to cultural resource management (CRM), so the Archaeologist's Toolkit focuses on practical approaches to solving real problems in CRM and

public archaeology. The books contain numerous case studies from
all parts of the continent, illustrating the range and diversity of applications. The series emphasizes the importance of such realistic
considerations as budgeting, scheduling, and team coordination. In
addition, accountability to the public as well as to the profession is a
common theme throughout the series.

Volume 1, *Archaeology by Design*, stresses the importance of research design in all phases and at all scales of archaeology. It shows
how and why you should develop, apply, and refine research designs.
Whether you are surveying quarter-acre cell tower sites or excavating
stratified villages with millions of artifacts, your work will be more
productive, efficient, and useful if you pay close and continuous attention to your research design.

Volume 2, *Archaeological Survey*, recognizes that most fieldwork
in North America is devoted to survey: finding and evaluating archaeological resources. It covers prefield and field strategies to help
you maximize the effectiveness and efficiency of archaeological survey. It shows how to choose appropriate strategies and methods ranging from landowner negotiations, surface reconnaissance, and shovel
testing to geophysical survey, aerial photography, and report writing.

Volume 3, *Excavation*, covers the fundamentals of dirt archaeology
in diverse settings, while emphasizing the importance of ethics during the controlled recovery—and destruction—of the archaeological
record. This book shows how to select and apply excavation methods
appropriate to specific needs and circumstances and how to maximize
useful results while minimizing loss of data.

Volume 4, *Artifacts*, provides students as well as experienced archaeologists with useful guidance on preparing and analyzing artifacts. Both prehistoric- and historic-era artifacts are covered in detail.
The discussion and case studies range from processing and cataloging
through classification, data manipulation, and specialized analyses of
a wide range of artifact forms.

Volume 5, *Archaeobiology*, covers the analysis and interpretation
of biological remains from archaeological sites. The book shows how
to recover, sample, analyze, and interpret the plant and animal remains most frequently excavated from archaeological sites in North
America. Case studies from CRM and other archaeological research
illustrate strategies for effective and meaningful use of biological
data.

Volume 6, *Curating Archaeological Collections*, addresses a crucial
but often ignored aspect of archaeology: proper care of the specimens

and records generated in the field and the lab. This book covers strategies for effective short- and long-term collections management. Case studies illustrate the do's and don'ts that you need to know to make the best use of existing collections and to make your own work useful for others.

Volume 7, *Presenting the Past*, covers another area that has not received sufficient attention: communication of archaeology to a variety of audiences. Different tools are needed to present archaeology to other archaeologists, to sponsoring agencies, and to the interested public. This book shows how to choose the approaches and methods to take when presenting technical and nontechnical information through various means to various audiences.

Each of these books and the series as a whole are designed to be equally useful to practicing archaeologists and to archaeology students. Practicing archaeologists in CRM firms, agencies, academia, and museums will find the books useful as reference tools and as brush-up guides on current concerns and approaches. Instructors and students in field schools, lab classes, and short courses of various types will find the series valuable because of each book's practical orientation to problem solving.

As the series editors, we have enjoyed bringing these books together and working with the authors. We thank all of the authors— Steve Black, Dave Carmichael, Terry Childs, Jim Collins, Charlie Ewen, Kevin Jolly, Robert Lafferty, Brian Molyneaux, Kris Sobolik, and Lynne Sullivan—for their hard work and patience. We also offer sincere thanks to Mitch Allen of AltaMira Press and a special acknowledgment to Brian Fagan.

WILLIAM GREEN
LARRY J. ZIMMERMAN

# ACKNOWLEDGMENTS

## David L. Carmichael

I would like to thank the colleagues and friends who have assisted me in the preparation of this volume. Researchers who have provided data and insights from their own projects include Steve Black, Peter Eidenbach, Lane Ellis, Mark Gutzman, Robert Hard, Gary Hebler, Rob Jackson, Lisa Meyer, Myles Miller, Yvonne Oakes, Gary Strobel, and Rick Wessel. Evelyn Chandler provided archival data on the archeological contracts at Eaker Air Force Base. We appreciate the patience and encouragement of the series editors, Larry Zimmerman and Bill Green. We would like to thank Scott Cutler of the El Paso Centennial Museum, Julie Hall of the U.S. Army Corps of Engineers, and Joan Oxendine of the U.S. Bureau of Land Management, California Desert District, for their assistance in securing permission to use illustrations previously published in contract reports.

## Robert H. Lafferty III

I received my early training in excavation methods from J. B. Graham during three summers of salvage archaeology for the University of Tennessee. He taught me how to carry out precise and accurate excavations, to use state-of-the-art technology, and to be aggressive in using innovative field methods. Jon D. Muller showed me how to use archeological data to test hypotheses while I was a graduate assistant at the Southern Illinois University field school. I am indebted to both of them, as well as scores of fellow students, who after seven field seasons prepared me to direct excavations successfully. This volume would not have been possible without the editorial assistance of my wife, Kathleen M. Hess, who turned my parts of the manuscript into coherent English. R. W. Maringer produced some of the graphics, and Kelly Sturtevant-Murdick helped with the bibliography. I thank all of them and the hundreds of crew members who have worked on the projects I have directed.

**Brian Leigh Molyneaux**

I would like to acknowledge Dr. Romas Vastokas, Peterborough, Ontario, who not only presided over my first formal dig at the Trent University Field School but also let me work on weekends, because I couldn't get enough of it. And I would like to thank the many field crews I have worked with, for tolerating my relentlessly cheerful demeanor. I owe most to my family, from my mom and dad to my wife and children, for letting me spend so many summers in northern Canada, when I should have been home, digging the garden!

# 1

# INTRODUCTION

> We cannot question seriously or effectively without reference to the past. Without the past there is no future for man, nor even a present being. All he is is the sum of his past, and all he can hope to become is written somewhere in this experience. To know the past is not necessarily to be bound by it, but some degree of knowledge can save a lot of wasted effort and set a frame for performance that gives life the meaning of shared human endeavor.
>
> *—Roderick Haig-Brown* (quoted in J. Taylor 1999)

Archaeology is unique in its ability to explore human behavior outside the limits of written records. History deals with past behavior as well, of course, but in most parts of the world, the time covered by historic documents represents a mere blink of an eye in the broad scope of the human experience. Many significant developments, such as the peopling of the New World, the development of plant and animal domestication, and the rise of complex social systems, occurred before the advent of writing. Some prehistoric phenomena have no surviving modern analogs that can be studied ethnographically. Moreover, archaeology not only allows us to study past behavior but also helps us see changes in behavior over time, or cultural evolution. We are able to measure the rates of culture change and to develop explanations to account for the observed changes.

Archaeologists most often realize this unique contribution to our understanding of the human condition through archaeological excavation. Excavating into the earth is traveling back in time, as we seek to expose soil layers containing the physical traces of the behavior of earlier human populations. Yet, archaeological excavation is much more than digging holes. It is recording and assembling a record of past behavior, giving meaning to that record, and applying the meanings in a wide variety of contexts, including academic research, education, land use planning, and public policy development. Each site and each feature we excavate is a potential window to the past. We use the collective record of such glimpses as the basis for understanding our development as a species. What we do throughout the excavation process affects our ability to explain our past and to meet the needs of society that require and justify excavation in the first place.

## ANOTHER EXCAVATION BOOK?

Why do we need another book on archaeological excavation techniques? A number of how-to books have been written in recent years, and more are in preparation. Many of them are more lengthy and comprehensive than this Toolkit volume; some contain quite good discussions of the logistical and mechanical aspects of conducting a traditional archaeological dig. Most such books give short shrift, however, to a range of topics and issues that archaeologists must face every day. Archaeology has changed a great deal in the past three decades. Significant advances have been made in the technology used in the field and laboratory. The research questions of interest today are often more complex than those of the past. The reasons for selecting sites to be excavated, and the very need for excavation, are driven by the interplay of growth and development, environmental law, and conservation ethics.

During a recent revision of the anthropology curriculum, the University of Texas at El Paso consulted colleagues and potential employers in the private sector to find out what skills they felt students should obtain to be readily employable after graduation. Not surprisingly, they said that many students lack significant fieldwork training and experience. While many students have coursework in archaeological methods, and some attend summer field schools, they don't usually experience fieldwork resembling the realities of most contemporary archaeology until graduate school. Perhaps more surprising was their observation that new graduates, even from large, established academic programs, generally lacked a basic understanding of the legal requirements and ethical considerations involved in the jobs they were seeking.

Clearly, these perceived needs reflect the changing circumstances of archaeology in the United States. Since the mid-1970s, the discipline has seen a proportional decrease in the amount of grant-supported academic archaeological research and a huge increase in publicly funded studies conducted in advance of development projects. Cultural resources management (CRM) now generates most of the funds spent on archaeology and employs most of the archaeologists doing research in the United States. However, for most professional archaeologists, the field techniques, legal knowledge, and ethical skills needed were acquired on the job; they are not generally taught in most archaeology curricula or textbooks.

Most archaeology texts discuss excavation methods as they might be used on a multiyear field school project, or what Barker (1996) refers to as research archaeology. In reality, most CRM projects are conducted more quickly, and very few extend beyond a single field season in duration. Yet, textbooks typically devote little space to the demands of such studies. In two popular texts, CRM and fieldwork ethics are covered in only seven or eight pages (Hester, Shafer, and Feder 1997; Renfrew and Bahn 1991:470–77). Barker (1996) devotes an entire chapter to CRM activities but treats them in a mildly off-handed way, as rescue and salvage operations, which are not quite real research efforts.

Nevertheless, Barker (1996:143) argues convincingly that rescue archaeology (i.e., CRM) requires at least as much skill and greater rigor than traditional academic archaeology. If so, it may be the case that archaeologists have not been fully preparing students for eventual employment in the CRM setting. Students and researchers need to be familiar with excavation techniques such as subsurface testing methods, maintaining excavation units, drawing stratigraphic profiles, mapping, and dating. But they should also understand the legal requirements of CRM, as well as their implications for project schedules and the choice of research methods. It is also important to be aware of the legal and ethical issues involved in client–contractor relationships, archaeological stewardship, and interactions with the interested public.

This volume touches on all these issues, albeit lightly. The full range of fieldwork details cannot be covered in a book of this length, and the reader should understand that no text can anticipate all field contingencies. Rather, the application of field techniques is a creative process, with different projects presenting different demands and opportunities. This book includes a series of case studies from excavations that illustrate the sorts of issues the reader may encounter in archaeology, as well as a range of possibilities to consider in addressing those issues. It is a book about methods, but it is also about attitudes and approaches.

## THEMATIC ORIENTATIONS

Although this volume is organized around case examples highlighting important issues in excavation, several additional overarching themes are intertwined with the discussions throughout the book. The reader is encouraged to consider these themes, discussed in the following sections, during all aspects and phases of excavation:

- CRM activities deserve our best efforts.
- Setting ethical priorities is a key aspect of modern archaeology.
- Archaeology is still part of anthropology.
- The scope of excavation activities should be warranted and appropriate.

## OUR BEST EFFORTS

Years ago, a fellow graduate student, now a professional colleague, remarked that archaeologists couldn't really justify their discipline as somehow being relevant to society. It is so esoteric, so unnecessary to society at large, that we should be thankful that people tolerate archaeology, and we should just go about our business. In today's research environment, such a view is untenable. Whether researchers are comfortable with the idea or not, archaeologists have many responsibilities beyond simply conducting good research (Lynott and Wylie 1995). Archaeology is no longer simply tolerated, it is required by law and paid for primarily with public funds. Federally mandated archaeological research costs between $70 and $100 million per year (Haas 1998; Knudson, McManamon, and Myers 1995:iii, 56–60; Renfrew and Bahn 1991:475), with others giving even higher estimates, so we really do need to be accountable to the public when taxpayer dollars support our research.

Of course, this is not the only way that archaeology is relevant to society. Like other parts of culture, our knowledge of the past is an instrument used to create meaning and order. Archaeology therefore plays a social and political role in the control and use of information about the past (Thomas 1991:46–47). For example, the determination of continuity in occupation or the cultural affiliation of sites may play a role in Native American land claim cases or the disposition of human remains recovered from those sites (Ucko 1989:xiii). Site characterization and the assessment of significance have had effects on the decisions to close military bases, with enormous impacts on neighboring communities. Public interpretation of archaeological research can affect local and regional tourism markets. The involvement of local residents in research can empower communities, build pride in cultural heritage, and spread the conservation ethic (Pyburn and Wilk 1995). Archaeological studies in general, and CRM in particular, demand and deserve our best efforts because the results do matter.

However, the key laws and regulations that structure CRM fairly narrowly define the impact of most archaeological work. At the federal level, the most important of these are the National Historic Preservation Act of 1966, as amended (NHPA), the Archaeological Resources Protection Act of 1979 (ARPA), and the Native American Graves Protection and Repatriation Act of 1990 (NAGPRA). For present purposes, it is sufficient to highlight a few key points.

Section 106 of the NHPA requires the proponents of federally funded or permitted development projects to identify, evaluate, and consider the effects of their actions on historic properties (significant archaeological, historical, or traditional cultural entities). Section 110 of the act directs federal land-managing agencies to inventory and evaluate the historic properties on their landholdings to facilitate their effective management. If a proposed federal project will have an adverse effect on a significant site, a common solution is to mitigate the effect by recovering data through excavation before the site is destroyed by construction. Most archaeological excavation activities in the United States are now done to meet one or the other of these needs: site characterization or data recovery.

Most such research is conducted by contractors affiliated with private firms or university research centers. Although federal agencies, tribes, or regulatory offices employ some archaeologists, most are involved with CRM as contractors. Despite their contribution to the discipline and the labor pool, it is important to remember that contractors have no formal role and no authority in the CRM compliance process. The federal agencies' representatives are the decision makers, and they are responsible for complying with federal laws. The main procedural functions for the archaeologist are to make recommendations to the decision makers regarding the significance of sites and the appropriateness of data recovery strategies.

Significance, as slippery as the concept may be (Tainter and Lucas 1983), is something we usually determine by evaluating an archaeological site's research potential. To justify destruction of a site (see chapter 3), we need to structure data recovery efforts to make the most of that research potential, but potential in relation to what? We must bring knowledge of current regional research issues and state-of-the-art technological capabilities to our studies, as our work will help determine whether sites survive or are destroyed. We need to justify site evaluations by regional research priorities; we need to articulate data recovery plans in research designs that we link to historic contexts. To do less than our best is to abdicate the main role archaeologists have in determining how archaeological sites in this country are managed and studied.

## SETTING ETHICAL PRIORITIES

Contemporary archaeologists have multiple ethical responsibilities relating to the various constituencies that are served by our work. These include the conservation ethic and a stewardship role in the public trust; the professional responsibility to meet standards of research; the need to provide cost-effective, justifiable research products for our clients; the need to provide adequate training for our students; and the responsibility to consider the effects of our research on Native Americans and members of other descendant communities. These various and sometimes conflicting demands provide ample opportunities for the development of ethical dilemmas. In fact, Fowler (1984:108) has suggested that the increase in archaeological contracting related to CRM has led to more ethical problems than any other recent development in American archaeology.

Many of these problems arise from the differences between the legitimate concerns of archaeologists, such as research goals and the conservation ethic, and project sponsors whose main objective is completion of the proposed development. Unlike that for other professionals, such as lawyers and engineers, the archaeologist's relationship with a client is not necessarily as clear as one might suppose. Many, perhaps most, project sponsors would prefer to proceed without doing any archaeological research, or at least minimizing the amount of work undertaken. But, if previous research in the region is lacking or inadequate to inform significance evaluations, a certain amount of work will be necessary to meet compliance requirements and, therefore, the client's needs. In other words, archaeologists will sometimes be in the position of informing or at least suggesting to a client what needs to be done, the reverse of what would be expected in most contracting situations. Moreover, many archaeologists would argue that their first responsibility is not to the client but to the public trust (as stewards of the archaeological record) or to indigenous peoples (because they are often the groups most affected by our research). As a result, archaeologists' recommendations can often reflect their own perceptions of the client's needs, not the client's perception of those needs.

Given the litigious nature of contemporary American law, it's not surprising that in response to a detailed proposal for consultation and data recovery on one of their projects, a client once asked, "What is our liability if we choose not to comply with the law?" Hopefully, most archaeologists will not encounter such attitudes very often, but they may be more common in business than we would like to think. A strong ethical stance is needed to advocate for the law, for the archaeological record, and to protect one's professional reputation. "Ethical responsibility is not beside the point of archaeology; it is the only thing that will keep our discipline alive" (Pyburn and Wilk 1995:76).

## ARCHAEOLOGY AS ANTHROPOLOGY

Engaging nonarchaeologists in dialogs about archaeological materials and in partnerships for their management represents real change in the discipline (Zimmerman 1995:65). Consultation and cooperation with Native Americans comprise a dimension of archaeology that goes beyond the "stones and bones" training that many of us received. Just the other day, an archaeologist related a recent conversation she had with a colleague regarding their experiences consulting with Native Americans. The colleague expressed admiration for those of us who work with tribal peoples: "It's so hard; I'm an archaeologist, not an anthropologist." Of course, at least in the United States, virtually all archaeologists receive their academic degrees in anthropology, so how is it that members of our discipline can come to view themselves as archaeologists, not anthropologists?

The effectiveness of our training is fully evident in the following statements overheard at the 1993 Annual Meeting of the Society for American Archaeology (SAA) in St. Louis: "Aren't the ethics of dealing with Native Americans pretty much self evident? There sure seem to be a lot of these sessions. The ethics for responding to Native American concerns may lead to censorship and the loss of my academic freedom. I went into archaeology so I wouldn't have to deal with living people." (See sidebar 1.1 for the story of how one of the authors entered the field of archaeology.)

## 1.1.   BECOMING AN ARCHAEOLOGIST

Although the details will differ from one individual to the next, the following scenario, an abbreviated version of David Carmichael's own career, may not be very different from how many of us were first drawn to the field and then socialized into the profession.

As a youth growing up in the suburbs of a large midwestern city, Carmichael decided early on that he would study archaeology. But, even earlier, his interest had focused on rocks. Or, more precisely, on rocks, minerals, fossils, and landforms—anything geological. He filled the crawlspace in his parents' home with rock specimens from all over the country, collected by the grocery bag full on summer family vacations. What strange caching behavior might a future archaeologist infer from this?

Then one summer, in fourth or fifth grade, while cultivating the backyard garden (the large one, before it was replaced by the garage), his hoe unearthed a chalcedony flake. Not surprising perhaps, in the rural farmlands, but pretty remarkable in the suburbs. What a revelation: Not only were there interesting rocks to be found right at home, but some of them had also been modified by humans! After spending much of the summer reading the anthropology books from the local public library, he became aware that the ancestors of today's American Indians made flaked stone tools and that flakes were their byproducts. In other words, he was drawn to the study of archaeological materials precisely because they are the products of the behavior of past Native American peoples.

How ironic that as he proceeded through his academic archaeological training, he was conditioned to view prehistoric artifacts not as the handiwork of Native Americans but as specimens, assemblages, foci, phases, branches, and material cultures. There was a hint of the dialog to come when, as an undergraduate in a western university, he became aware of the double standard in the laws relating to the treatment of human remains. It was against the law to remove bones from a marked cemetery in a ghost town, but it was all right to remove Indian remains from unmarked graves at prehistoric pueblos. Indeed, it must be important to do so, for the museum was full of them. Like the material culture items in the museum collections, the Indian remains were treated as specimens, not as the ancestors of living Native Americans.

But it was not until much later, after graduate school, that it became clear to the now-professional archaeologist how detached most of us were from the Native American essence of much of the archaeological record. As a result of his involvement in CRM research for a client working in the Northern Plains, Carmichael had the opportunity to do archaeology in a region with a large Native American population and numerous living traditions. Presumed tipi rings make up a large proportion of the archaeological features studied in that region, and he was sure that the local indigenous peoples would be able to contribute to our understanding of them. Yet, he found entire published volumes devoted to such features containing hardly a mention of ethnoarchaeology or Native American views (Ives 1986; Wilson et al. 1981). In fact, our archaeologist found a persistent, semiconscious exclusion of contemporary Native Americans from considerations of the archaeological record. For example, in Montana and Wyoming, some researchers have developed a shorthand terminology to describe archaeological sites that distinguishes *aboriginal* (Native American) sites from *historic* (Euroamerican) sites. Granted, it may be difficult, sometimes impossible, to distinguish late prehistoric tipi ring sites from historic period tipi ring sites, and this classification makes some sense on morphological grounds. However, it also embodies the idea that historic sites are Euroamerican and that modern Indian populations are not connected to the archaeology of their ancestors. Of course, this suggestion is false, but it does reflect a widely held perception among archaeologists.

In 1989, Carmichael went to the World Archaeological Congress meetings on Archaeological Ethics and the Treatment of the Dead, held in South Dakota. Not many American archaeologists attended this conference. Those who did attend often had to endure being yelled at by Native Americans; evidently, someone (actually, a lot of people) had a different kind of interest in *our* archaeological materials, and many researchers didn't yet realize it.

It is ironic that while many archaeologists practice archaeology because of an interest in prehistoric Indians, most have never worked with Native Americans, and many would rather not do so. Recent relations between archaeologists and Native Americans have often been adversarial, especially in the context of reburial and repatriation issues (Echo-Hawk and Echo-Hawk 1991; Echo-Hawk 1993). With the passage of NAGPRA, the status of Indians has begun to shift from being specimens or subjects to being partners in research. This development has been so unsettling to some researchers that it has been blamed for the demise of archaeology as a discipline (Meighan 1992a, 1992b, 1993, 1994). Is archaeology really going out of business? Probably not, but as Jonathan Haas (1993) remarked, the days of doing archaeology as we have for the last hundred years are over.

The discipline is changing, to address new levels of accountability and to accommodate collaborative approaches to understanding the past (Salazar and Barrow 2000; Magne 1997; Parker and Bevitt 1997; Swidler et al. 1997; Watkins and Parry 1997). By recognizing the valid concerns and insights Native Americans bring to such collaborations, archaeologists can gain new understandings about the past (Zimmerman 1995:66) and the living traditions that maintain them (see sidebar 6.5 for the story of a site that illustrates this point). New requirements to consult with members of traditional cultures should not be viewed as impediments to research. Isn't consultation something we should be doing with any community, traditional or not? Consultation provides opportunities to enhance and expand our knowledge of the human condition. It has been said "success is a journey, not a destination." In our discipline, one might say, "archaeology is a process of knowing, not simply digging holes." Archaeology is still part of anthropology, and there is much to be learned.

## APPROPRIATE EXCAVATION

Providing our best efforts in archaeology, regardless of whether or not the project is related to CRM, does not necessarily mean doing everything that is possible at a site. Often, it will mean doing what is necessary (under the law, in relation to our research design, etc.), what is appropriate, and what is reasonable. The importance of a site is often determined by the presence or absence of intact subsurface deposits, as they relate directly to research potential (but see chapter 3). The (subsurface vs. surface) extent or boundary must be identified if one is to adequately describe a historic property for NRHP nomination.

All states are by now supposed to have in place master planning documents that summarize the existing knowledge and research priorities for each region and time period in the state (King 1977:93–94). Arkansas has one of the best such documents, *A State Plan for the Conservation of Archaeological Resources in Arkansas* (Davis 1982). One portion of the plan contains standards for fieldwork, including details of the number and sorts of test excavation units that might be

## 1.2. THE EAKER SITE

One of the most interesting archaeological projects Carmichael and Lafferty have worked on involves the Eaker site (3MS105), located on Eaker Air Force Base in northeastern Arkansas. The Eaker site is a large, multicomponent village covering thirty hectares (seventy-five acres) along the Pemiscot Bayou on the Mississippi River floodplain (Lafferty and Cande 1989). Artifacts recovered at the site include materials of the Woodland period Barnes and Baytown traditions, and a Middle Mississippian occupation. However, most of the site is attributable to the Late Mississippian Nodena phase, placing it among the fourteen largest Mississippian sites in the country. Subsurface deposits at the site are complex and well preserved; identified features include palisade trenches, a leveled mound, middens, burials, and an estimated four hundred to five hundred buried houses. The Eaker site is part of an important cluster of thirty-four sites near Blytheville, Arkansas (Morse and Morse 1983:289), but unlike other sites in the area, 3MS105 has been protected from looting since the 1940s by its inclusion in Eaker Air Force Base.

Most of what we know about the Eaker site is a direct result of the research undertaken at Eaker Air Force Base in the context of the proposed Peacekeeper Rail Garrison Program. Archaeological research at the site was conducted by archaeological contractors under subcontract to Tetra Tech, Inc., of San Bernardino, California, an environmental consulting firm working for the air force. The circumstances surrounding initiation of research at the site are presented here as an illustration of how contemporary CRM archaeology demands a knowledge of legal requirements for compliance, ethical concerns for our clients, and the application of state-of-the-art techniques to the research opportunities presented.

Archaeologists at Tetra Tech prepared a detailed scope of work for the initial investigation based on an understanding of project parameters, time schedules, and compliance requirements. Specifically, it was necessary to evaluate the site's significance, or eligibility for the National Register of Historic Places (NRHP). To meet this need, studies at the Eaker site were designed to identify the perimeter of the site, assess the dates and types of prehistoric use of the site, and determine the nature and depth of buried cultural deposits.

Potential subcontractors submitted bids calling for as many as 12,550 shovel tests. But, in an effort to minimize unnecessary damage to the site, and with the concurrence of the SHPO, such bids were rejected in favor of remote sensing accompanied by small-scale test excavations.

For the record, the level of effort outlined in the request for proposals (RFP) was sufficient to define and evaluate the site. Instead of making Swiss cheese of the site, the remote sensing helped identify a complex matrix of preserved subsurface features at depths of 18 to 133 centimeters (mostly below the depths reached by shovel testing) while minimizing damage to the deposits (see chapter 4). The Eaker site was successfully listed on the NRHP in 1993 and was designated a National Historic Landmark in 1996.

warranted at different kinds of sites. While the utility of such a well-conceived plan cannot be easily overstated, the tendency may be for some researchers to follow the detailed procedures like a cookbook. The guidelines themselves provide a cautionary note against this approach.

Given the geomorphology and ground cover of the region, significance evaluations would normally involve extensive subsurface testing, using techniques such as shovel tests, auger holes, coring, or test pits. The guidelines call for shovel tests or auger holes to be placed every five to thirty meters, depending on artifact densities and surface visibility. On a very large site, however, that sampling interval could result in the excavation of tens of thousands of shovel tests, with the testing constituting a major impact to site integrity. In consultation with the state historic preservation officer (SHPO), other approaches may be negotiated, such as using nondestructive remote sensing in lieu of most of the test excavation that would normally be undertaken pursuant to state guidelines (see chapter 4). The resulting scope of work might call for surface mapping, remote sensing, and some small-scale coring and test pit excavations to verify the magnetometer results. You need to be aware of situations that call for variances from guidelines (sidebar 1.2).

Preparing proposals that are beyond the scope of work is not an adaptive strategy for most archaeological contractors, as potential clients are likely to select thc more responsive proposals. However, it is even more disconcerting that experienced researchers would propose a level of effort based on what was customary, not what was warranted and appropriate.

## CONCLUSIONS

Archaeology is an exciting undertaking. Despite the potentially tedious individual tasks that comprise archaeological research, the excavation of material remains of the past can inform us about the human condition in ways that cannot be accomplished through any other means. Ultimately, we are studying human behavior, not features and artifacts. House floors, pottery sherds, and stone tools are the indirect indicators of those behaviors, not ends in themselves. As archaeologists, we should ask ourselves often what we are doing and why. If we remain focused on our ultimate goal of understanding human behavior, of doing the anthropology of past societies, we will be reminded that our work matters. Others care about the past, and others are affected by our research. We shouldn't propose or conduct a certain level of effort or a certain approach simply because it is customary. We should do so because it is necessary and warranted, thereby doing archaeology by design, not by default (see Toolkit, volume 1).

## ORGANIZATION OF THE VOLUME

Details of the excavation activities at the Eaker site and several other interesting sites will be discussed, usually in sidebars, throughout this book. Examples come from a variety of locations and a range of site types, presenting issues, answers, and techniques that might relate to research opportunities throughout the country. Chapter 2 presents an overview of the history of archaeological excavation in the Americas and beyond. In chapter 3, we will explore the inherently destructive nature of archaeological research. Given this reality, our work can and should be justifiable in terms of research goals and ethical considerations. Also included is a consideration of ways to control the destruction by maintaining control of artifact and feature provenience within a site.

Site characterization and test excavation techniques are discussed in chapter 4. We will revisit the Eaker site to examine the results of test excavations. Traditional hand excavation techniques are compared with mechanical trenching as a basic search strategy. Chapter 5 considers data recovery. Chapter 6 discusses the treatment of special samples for dating, flotation techniques, and the treatment of human remains, including reburial. In a way, the development of these specialized techniques reflects the changes in the discipline as a whole, so at the end of chapter 6 we consider the future of excavation.

Much of what we do as field archaeologists today has a substantial history, and our techniques changed substantially as archaeology grew into a scientific discipline. What follows in chapter 2 is abbreviated history of archaeological methods, with broad geographic coverage.

# 2

# EXCAVATION

## A BRIEF HISTORY

W e have two kinds of empirical data in archaeology," W. W. Taylor lectured in his last method and theory class. "We have artifacts with their physical and chemical specification, and we have their locations in space. All else is inference."

It was the spring of 1974, and Southern Illinois University was on the forefront of the "New Archaeology" that was sweeping the nation. But whether deduction or inference was used to impute meaning to the results, Taylor had hit the empirical nail on the head. What distinguishes archaeology from pothunting is that we know where the artifacts came from. Using precise spatial information on artifact context, we can deduce or infer patterns of cultural behavior and evolutionary trajectories of technologies. These concerns govern the conduct of archaeology to the current day, and they certainly inform and even direct how we dig.

Spatial control, or provenience, of artifacts recovered in the field is critical in excavations and is one of the most powerful tools we have for investigating archaeological deposits. With good spatial control, we can tell what groups of artifacts came before another group of artifacts, and we can tell that one area of a site was used for a temple, and another was the place where canoes were made. Some kinds of analysis require spatial precision of millimeters, and other kinds require much less precision, on the order of hundreds of meters. The hallmark of modern archaeological excavation is the use of a three-dimensional X, Y, Z Cartesian grid. This grid is easily manipulated using standard mathematics, makes precise measurement easy, and can be tied into regional Geographical Information Systems (GIS) analysis.

Looters merely obtain artifacts from the ground. Archaeology does have its roots in such activities in the eighteenth and nineteenth centuries when the European empires plundered the classical antiquities of the Mediterranean, but such activities are no longer acceptable. In this chapter, we review the development of excavation and related analysis techniques as a means of defining certain basic concepts. This history focuses on the development of the techniques of spatial control, the essence of modern excavations.

## THE EMERGENCE OF PROVENIENCE CONTROL

The first part of the nineteenth century saw the emergence of maps and scaled drawings that gave some provenience control, though only for large architectural elements. Austin Layard conducted the excavation of the Royal Assyrian palace at Nimrud during the 1840s (Layard 1849). His book, a best-seller, has maps of his excavations that show the location of the specific architectural remains (figure 2.1). Letters key rooms, and numbers identify architectural elements, which were enumerated in appendices. (Presumably, he also numbered the artifacts.) He also included scaled drawings of some of the architectural elements. A major find was the royal archives, containing thousands of texts in an undeciphered cuneiform script accidentally preserved by being fired when the palace burned. Three readable Egyptian hieroglyphic inscriptions were discovered as well, allowing the texts to be cross-dated to the Egyptian dynastic chronology that was rapidly being deciphered from the monuments and papyri. Suddenly, datable archaeological contexts in Mesopotamia were extended back in time, from 600 B.C. to 3000 B.C. Many of the accounts in the Bible, once thought to be mythical, were given a new reality as the capitals of many of the legendary cities were investigated over the next century. Investigators were beginning to grasp the importance of provenience as the meaning of finding an Egyptian text in the Euphrates began to sink in: These distant monarchs were corresponding with each other. This was meaningful provenience on a regional scale of hundreds of kilometers.

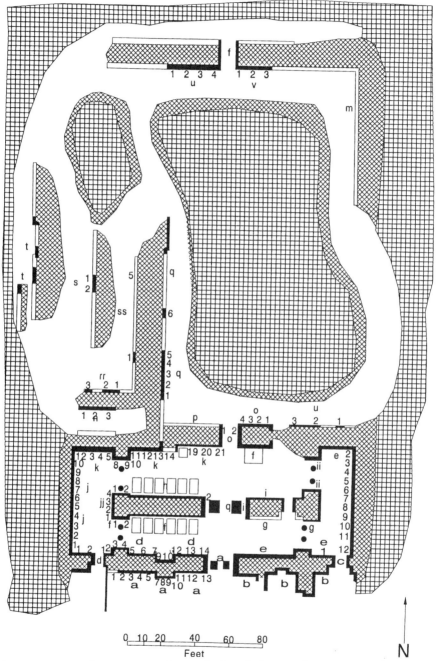

**Figure 2.1.** Layard's 1849 map of part of Nimrud showing the excavation plan. Room parts are lettered, and the specific architectural elements are numbered. (After Layard 1849: 35.)

Meanwhile, back in England, General Augustus Henry Pitt Rivers was developing methods of three-dimensional spatial control that would change archaeology into a science capable of dealing with prehistoric sites. He had been intrigued by the concept of progress in the 1851 exposition. The idea of progress was an early form of cultural evolutionism that saw a progression of forms leading in a unilineal fashion through stages of development that culminated in the current pinnacle of evolutionary success, Victorian Europe. This was used as a justification for the formation of empires. Pitt Rivers began collecting weapons by type to illustrate their technological development. His interest in technological development led him to excavate sites with a precision almost unparalleled today, piece-plotting even the smallest artifacts. His excavations on the Roman fortifications at Crissbury Hill Fort (1875) in southeastern England discovered a distinctive kind of pottery under the fortification wall, leading to the realization that these ceramics predated the construction of the fort. He excavated the twelve-foot-deep fortification ditch (figure 2.2), where he documented artifacts in obvious strata, then left the ditches open and reexcavated parts of them later to get data on infilling rates. About 1882, he inherited the 27,700-acre Pitt Rivers estate and began excavation in earnest. He documented this work in four lavishly illustrated quarto volumes (Pitt Rivers 1887–1898).

Pitt Rivers's procedures, including piece plotting and stratigraphic excavation, were so much more detailed than his colleagues' methods that he perceived that they thought him "eccentric" (Fagan 1985:103). However, his ideas were so current (Tylor's [1871] evolutionary theory was the academic rage) and his results so remarkable that he could not be ignored. He was tremendously influential on the young generation of archaeologists then in training, including Leonard Woolley, Flinders Petrie, Mortimer Wheeler, and Howard Carter, who would be on the forefront of developing his methods into a new archaeology. These Britons, as well as Heinrich Schliemann and others, employed stratigraphy, seriation, and cross-dating as tools to understand archaeological deposits, sites, and cultures.

*Stratigraphy* is perhaps the principal concept employed in archaeological excavation. Pitt Rivers borrowed the concept from geology. Stratigraphy is based on the law of superposition, which holds that layers above are more recent than those beneath; that is, the layer on

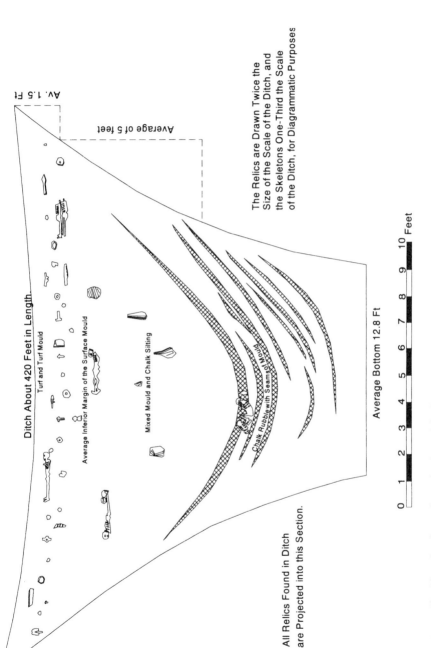

Ditch About 420 Feet in Length.

Av. 1.5 Ft

Average of 5 feet

Turf and Turf Mould

Average Inferior Margin of the Surface Mould

Mixed Mould and Chalk Silting

Chalk Rubble with Seams of Mould

All Relics Found in Ditch are Projected into this Section.

The Relics are Drawn Twice the Size of the Scale of the Ditch, and the Skeletons One-Third the Scale of the Ditch, for Diagrammatic Purposes

Average Bottom 12.8 Ft

0  1  2  3  4  5  6  7  8  9  10  Feet

Figure 2.2.  Pitt Rivers's schematic projection of the levels of the point plotted artifacts recovered from Wor Barrow moat. (After Wheeler 1954:26.)

the bottom is the oldest. In geological terms, strata usually span hundreds of kilometers, but at the scale of archaeological sites, the strata are, at most, several hundred meters wide or long. Nevertheless, the principle holds, with very few exceptions. Interpreting sequences built by stratigraphic analysis gives time depth to archaeological deposits.

*Seriation* refers to chronological ordering of archaeological units using changes in style or technology through time (see Toolkit, volume 4; also Lyman, O'Brien, and Dunnell 1997). Flinders Petrie (1901), working in Egypt, developed the first application when he tried to chronologically order hundreds of predynastic and early dynastic graves. Petrie's work extended the Egyptian relative chronology several thousand years into prehistory.

Petrie found two wares of Mycenaen pottery in twelfth- and eighteenth-dynasty contexts of known age, thereby dating those wares (Rapport and Wright 1964:183). This is an example of using an artifact type as a *horizon marker*. These are distinctive artifacts that have very wide spatial distributions and were produced for only a short period of time. Sites in different regions can be cross-dated on the basis of such horizon markers.

## NORTH AMERICAN DEVELOPMENTS

The development of excavation methods in North America was similar to that in the Old World (Willey and Sabloff 1993). Thomas Jefferson was one of the earliest-documented excavators (Heizer 1959:218–21). He excavated a mound in 1784 to determine whether it was a mass grave from a battle, a place for reburial, or a town sepulcher. He cut a trench through the mound, described its stratigraphy, and documented the conditions of jumbled masses of bones at different levels. He observed that the burials on the top were less decayed and concluded that the mound was built through a series of periodic reburials. Jefferson's work was a precocious example of a modern approach to archaeology.

The driving impetus for subsequent excavation was to fill museums with artifacts, but there was also a specific research problem to investigate. After the American explorers and colonists crossed the Appalachian Mountains, they found large earthworks. Some conceived of a race of Moundbuilders who built the earthworks prior to the arrival of the Indians. Although there was much discussion about this "theory" and others that attributed the earthworks to lost Vikings, lost Welshmen, and the lost tribes of Israel, most serious investigators were fairly certain that Indians built the earthworks (Williams 2001).

In the 1880s, John Wesley Powell, director of the Bureau of American Ethnology (BAE), received money from Congress for surveys and excavations at mound sites of the eastern United States to test the Moundbuilder myth. Some of the BAE-affiliated excavators kept careful records and made excellent site maps. Cyrus Thomas (1894) reported his results in the twelfth annual report of the BAE. This report and the BAE would loom large in the archaeology of the following century.

Some investigators were better than others. The best excavators prepared site plans of the mounds. Some of these are the best maps we have of many of the large sites. Thomas summarized the contents of different mounds and sites and, for the most part, recorded artifact provenience only to the site level. By showing that Indians had built the burial mounds, he largely quashed the Moundbuilder myth. The resulting collections led to the first areal synthesis of eastern United States ceramics (Holmes 1903) and many other studies.

For the next several decades, Thomas's methods were the model, and data recovery was at the site level. Large museums sponsored numerous excavations, many of which recognized pit features and at least rudimentary stratigraphy (Mills 1907; Fowke 1922). Most of this work was in the Southwest, and it was there that the next major advances in the science of excavation took place.

In 1916, Nels Nelson, familiar with Pitt Rivers's work (O'Brien 1996:156), published an article in *American Anthropologist* on excavations he had carried out for the American Museum of Natural History at the Tano Ruins in New Mexico (Nelson 1916). His discoveries and methods would shake New World archaeology. Nelson cut *volumetrically controlled units* (excavation levels of the same volume or of known volume so that the quantity of artifacts can be meaningfully compared) out of a four-meter-thick profile of the midden adjacent to the Tano Pueblo. He divided the recovered sherds into different "types" based on perceived attributes and plotted their distribution by excavation level. Doing so demonstrated the presence of stratified habitation sites in North America and introduced volumetric quantification into archaeology. The former would in short order lead to spectacular discoveries of stratified deposits, but the latter would take several decades to seep into mainline archaeology. In 1919, the University of Arizona offered the first field school in archaeology (Gifford and Morris 1985). A. V. Kidder's excavations at Pecos Pueblo between 1915 and 1922 uncovered very deeply stratified deposits (figure 2.3; Kidder 1962). Kidder excavated a trench into the talus slope of the mesa, assuming that the most recent town fortification wall was on the edge of the mesa. The talus was much larger than Kidder had imagined. He had expected the work to take one season, but after two seasons, there was no end in sight. What he had thought was one ruin was at least six superimposed towns with defensive walls buried as much as seven meters deep. Kidder reserved large blocks for careful stratigraphic excavations. From the photographs, the blocks appear to be divided into 3 × 3–foot units with six- to twelve-inch cuts. The stratigraphic sequence allowed Kidder to define changes through time in ceramic styles. He confirmed and expanded Nelson's sequence at Tano, located only several miles away. It seemed clear to Kidder that the length of the pueblo period was much longer than previously suspected. How much earlier the human occupation began was about to be discovered.

During several summers, Kidder invited colleagues to Pecos to see and discuss the excavations and results. The Pecos Conference turned into an annual gathering, the first regional archaeological conference. It was no accident that Kidder was chairman of the Committee on State Archaeological Surveys of the National Research Council, which was trying to establish state, regional, and national archaeological organizations. At these conferences, archaeologists compared potsherds and results from their latest excavations, which accelerated the spread of new techniques of excavation. From that time forward, in the Southwest, excavations were increasingly conducted using volumetric control, and these techniques spread to the Southeast in the 1930s.

## DIRECT ASSOCIATION AND THE SEARCH FOR EARLY HUMANS IN THE NEW WORLD

In 1926, J. D. Figgins of the Denver Museum of Natural History was seeking evidence for the antiquity of humans in the New World. At the Folsom site in New Mexico, George McJunkin discovered a spear point in direct association with bones of extinct Pleistocene bison (from the Ice Ages in which the period from forty thousand to ten

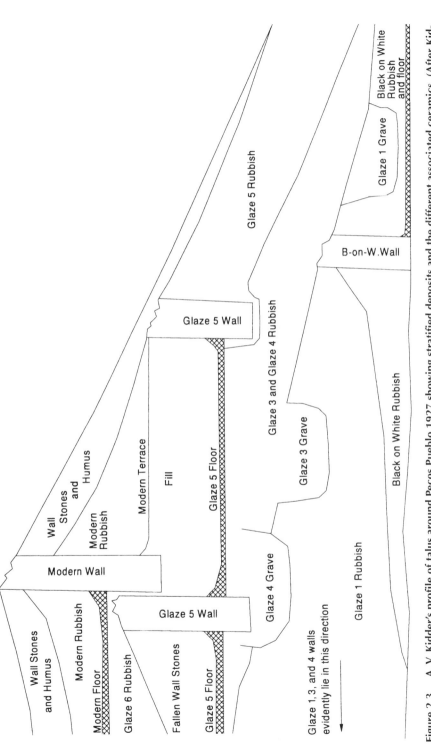

Figure 2.3.  A. V. Kidder's profile of talus around Pecos Pueblo 1927 showing stratified deposits and the different associated ceramics. (After Kidder 1962:103.)

thousand years ago is the probable time of human entry to the Americas) (Figgins 1927; Wormington 1964 has an engaging account of this discovery). This was such an important association that Figgins photographed the point and associated bones and removed it as a block to his laboratory. Over the following winter, he tried to convince colleagues of the authenticity of the associations. Some accepted his evidence, but others would rather have seen the point firmly embedded in the skull before they would accept the evidence. Figgins continued working and found a point firmly embedded between two ribs. He stopped the excavations and called all interested colleagues to the site. Archaeologists from all over the country dropped what they were doing and rushed to see the find *in situ* (a find still in place in the context where it was deposited). They were convinced. Figgins's precise careful excavation techniques and precise recording techniques changed American archaeology forever. His documentation of the artifact association to the nearest millimeter was of significance.

## THE GRID

At southwestern pueblo sites, it became standard practice to excavate through the prehistoric construction debris and midden deposits until room walls could be defined, at which point excavation switched to the clearing of individual rooms. In the East, sites seldom have rooms indicated on the surface, prompting use of grids for within-site control. *Grids* are units of regular size and shape laid out over a site in order to locate items conveniently in relation to each other. While the earliest use of grids was by Charles Peabody in his 1903 excavations at Jacobs Cave in Missouri (O'Brien 1996:158–69), it was not until the late 1920s that grids became routinely used in excavations. The shift to the use of grids is evident on site maps of the time, as excavations transform from round holes to a square-patterned grids. Claflin's (1931) excavations on Stalling's Island between 1921 and 1929 actually show this transition. The rectangular grid trenches are from the 1929 Harvard excavations, and the round pits and trenches were earlier.

The University of Chicago anthropology department, under the leadership of Fay-Cooper Cole (see Cole et al. 1951), played a pivotal role in the development and dissemination of the use of grids on archaeological sites. Cole started the Chicago field school in the 1920s. The first field school in the East, it was extremely influential because it trained many students who became leading archaeologists. Cole lectured on field methods at the first Southeastern Archaeology Conference, held in 1932 in Birmingham, Alabama. He advocated total recovery, even the recovery of items for which researchers had no immediate use, such as carbon and snail shells. The best way to recover everything was to grid the site into conveniently sized units, such as five-foot squares, and collect everything in a block sliced horizontally with a razor-sharp shovel. This became known as the "Chicago method" (figure 2.4). The meeting helped establish methods

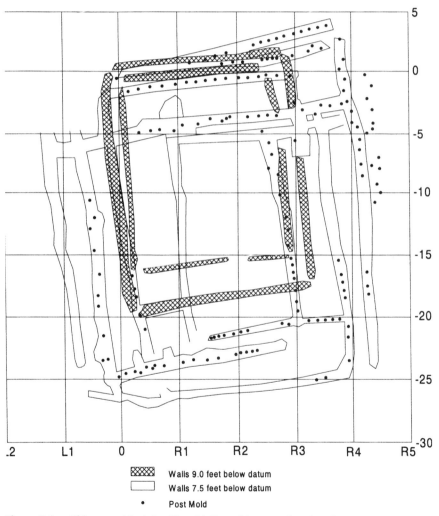

Walls 9.0 feet below datum
Walls 7.5 feet below datum
• Post Mold

**Figure 2.4.** Chicago grid at the Kincaid Site of Mxv1A showing the superimposed wall trenches. (After Cole et al. 1951:45.)

for the large archaeological projects of the Works Progress Administration (WPA) in the 1930s, which put thousands of people to work excavating sites throughout the Southeast. The collections resulting from these WPA projects still contain artifacts and samples that are of great importance today.

The "Chicago grid" was set up in feet and staked at five- or ten-foot intervals. A base line was run through the approximate center of the site. Parallel lateral lines were labeled L1-$n$ and R1-$n$ (left or right 1-$n$), and the other axis was labeled by plus or minus feet. This procedure made it possible to label each unit uniquely, such as L1-5, based on the designation of the southwest corner. Its application in the Southeast came just in time to record the large amounts of data generated when the WPA excavations began in earnest in 1934. The use of grids reached as far west as Nebraska by 1939 (see Hill and Kivett 1949).

## THEORETICAL DEVELOPMENTS

In 1948, W. W. Taylor published his Harvard dissertation, *A Study of Archeology*, in which he analyzed Americanist archaeology and compared what practitioners said they were doing with what they were actually doing. He concluded that, while archaeologists said they were doing anthropology, most were in fact doing historiography. Taylor's polemic stance led him to become essentially ostracized by most of the profession, although he received thirteen National Science Foundation grants to pursue his conjunctive approach to archaeology in the dry bluff shelters of northern Mexico.

During his senior year in college, Lafferty found a copy of Taylor's *A Study of Archaeology* in a bookstore. After reading it, he asked his archaeology professor why he had never been told about this very important work, which laid out some methods that could be employed to find and define cultural patterns. Lafferty was admonished, "We do not talk about him among our people." In January 1968, he chose to attend graduate school at Southern Illinois University because Taylor was teaching there. He enrolled in Taylor's very challenging course on Old World archaeology. Taylor was terrifyingly frank in his comments in class and expected the same of everyone else. However, after one student's presentation in a methods and theory class in which the student had been very critical of a senior archaeologist, Taylor told the student, "You can say it that way, if you want to spend the next twenty years talking to yourself. . . . I know." He was also very thorough, reading every paper three times, once to get a general sense, once for English, and finally making detailed comments on content. Lafferty got excellent feedback from Taylor. He eventually was offered the chance to work with Taylor in northern Mexico, but the draft board decided he should visit Vietnam instead. After his return in 1971, he found that the world of archaeology had changed.

Lewis Binford led the new archaeology of the 1960s and 1970s. Southern Illinois University (SIU) was on the edge of this wave because Taylor, the prophet, was there and because Binford briefly worked at SIU. Carmichael also received early exposure to the New Archaeology, at the University of New Mexico (UNM), where Binford was teaching and where Taylor's book was required reading. Binford (1962) argued in an influential article entitled "Archaeology as Anthropology" that archaeologists should be doing anthropology. That is, they should be working on defining and explaining cultural processes, rather than simply generating descriptions of past cultures and sequences of descriptions of past cultures.

In his classes at UNM, Binford's critique of traditional archaeology was incisive and often polemic. He argued that our primary challenge in interpreting the past is generally *not* any inherent limitations in the archaeological record but, rather, our ability to ask useful questions of it. "The material record does not speak forth self-evident truths," he would say. Knowledge proceeds from warranted arguments, not by appeal to authority; even well-known senior archaeologists could be wrong! There are no data except in response to research questions. Archaeologists always ask such questions, either implicitly or explicitly, the latter being preferable so we can more readily evaluate our ideas about how the world works (i.e., how the material record was formed). While analogy is important to archaeological interpretation, archaeologists should not feel bound by specific historical (i.e., ethnographic) analogies because prehistory encompasses many events and processes that lack modern or historic analogs.

The New Archaeology prompted archaeologists to be concerned about sampling and sampling design. Questions about consistency of samples led to the adaptation of screening. Screening had been done sporadically since the 1930s, when the Lower Mississippi Valley Survey began screening samples to assure consistency. In the early 1970s, systematically screened samples became the standard over much of North America. Another innovation of the late 1960s and the 1970s was the use of controlled surface collections to sample plow zone deposits. These kinds of collections can tell much about the structure of a site, as discussed in volume 2 of the Archaeologist's Toolkit series.

## THE BEGINNINGS OF CRM

During the 1950s and 1960s, much of the archaeological excavation being conducted in the country was salvage work in the lakes and reservoirs that were rapidly being built. This salvage work was partially modeled on the earlier WPA projects, but with smaller crews of only ten to twenty persons. The Smithsonian Institution ran the River Basin Survey and excavated many large sites in the Missouri River basin on the Plains. The National Park Service administered other salvage programs that were conducted by university departments of anthropology or museums. Usually, the sole archaeologist in the state conducted this work. This process changed radically after 1966 (see Toolkit, volume 1).

Perhaps two aspects of CRM archaeology should be highlighted here because of the effects they have on how excavations are conducted. First is the change in how sites are selected for excavation. For years it was customary to conduct excavations at the largest, most visible sites in a region to maximize the recovery of diagnostic artifacts, record the longest stratigraphic sequences, or interpret prominent sites for the public. Conversely, in CRM archaeology the study areas, and therefore the sites available for consideration, are typically determined by the extent of the proposed project. As a result, archaeologists have been forced to evaluate and excavate many smaller or less visible sites that were overlooked in the past. This has been a good thing, as these classes of sites have much to tell us about settlement patterns and the diversity of prehistoric adaptive strategies. Indeed, even in parts of the Southwest and Southeast, where excavations have been under way for more than a century, new information is gained from almost every excavation.

The other major change involves the recognition of multiple constituents and consumers of archaeological research. In addition to our colleagues, we now answer to government regulators, agency administrators, private sector clients, and the public. Clearly, the public includes a variety of ethnic groups, but a few groups have special connections to the archaeological record. The most important of these are Native Americans. Unfortunately, for much of the past two or three decades, relations between Native Americans and archaeologists have often been adversarial, due largely to disagreements over the disposition of human remains and associated artifacts. The passage of the Native American Graves Protection and Repatriation Act of 1990 (NAGPRA) substantially revised the relationship between archaeologists and Native Americans. Native American groups now have a formal role in deciding whether and how human remains will be studied and whether they will be reburied. These issues directly affect how excavations are conducted and how skeletal remains are treated in the field and laboratory.

## THE REAL INDIANA JONES

Indiana Jones, realized in the personification of the swashbuckling archaeologist, seems to have captured the popular imagination, perhaps even inspiring some among us to pursue archaeology. As W. W. Taylor also said in his lectures, we should pay attention to our metaphors because they sometimes become tenets of science. Some of the footage from *Raiders of the Lost Ark* metaphorically spans the transition from using no spatial control to detailed mapping. Jones is essentially looting when he grabs the golden idol and runs, with a very large stone ball rolling after him. Yet it took precise spatial control under stressful conditions to place the Staff of Ra (which also had to be exactly the right height) in exactly the right spot on the correct day and at the correct time to find the ark's location. Then he had to translate that location into the Germans' grid of the site of Tanis to find the ark.

Archaeological excavation demands precise recovery of spatial information under demanding (or even nasty) field conditions. One must make careful observations and accurate measurements and get them down on paper while the sweat is dripping on the paper or as one's fingers are shaking with cold. Snakes, scorpions, and other vermin are real obstacles, though seldom in the quantities Indy encounters. One of us (R.H.L.) once had to hold off the looters of the past at gunpoint. Another (D.L.C.) has witnessed field crews threatened at gunpoint in Texas and Illinois because of the imagined transgressions of CRM clients.

Indiana Jones is a Hollywood creation, but the physical stress he portrays is real in archaeology, and the rewards of excavating the long-lost residue of everyday life can be every bit as exciting as finding the Ark of the Covenant. Even more exciting is seeing, understanding, or elegantly describing a cultural pattern or a previously unperceived scientific abstraction.

Modern archaeology owes a great deal to the real archaeologists who paved the way with genius and a willingness to experiment with new approaches that gave them increasingly more sophisticated spatial and temporal control in their excavations. They recognized early on that archaeology is as destructive a process as looting if done without systematic approaches to excavation. The subject of the next chapter, which gets right to the heart of the matters of stewardship and conservation of archaeological sites, is about the attitudes we bring to our work and the obligations we owe as scientists to our publics.

## 3

# ARCHAEOLOGICAL EXCAVATION IS CONTROLLED DESTRUCTION

E xcavation is inherently a destructive activity. Archaeological excavation differs from looting and other kinds of digging because of the motivation for excavation, the methods used, and the treatment of the resulting collections.

It is a professional responsibility for archaeologists to be familiar with the Indiana Jones movies, if for no other reason than to understand the stereotypes and misunderstandings nonarchaeologists often have about what we do. The movies also provide a point of departure for considering what archaeology is and how it should be done. For the most part, what passes for archaeology in the movies would be considered looting by today's standards. Images of hundreds of laborers flinging dirt in every direction may seem romantic to the average viewer, but they represent poorly controlled excavation, which would result in the loss of most of the information available at the site. Of course, the "bad guys" are merely treasure hunting, but even Indiana Jones brings back a few gold ornaments wrapped in a scarf to sell to the museum to underwrite his expedition—looting, by today's standards. Nevertheless, digging and the removal of artifacts are part of even the most cautious archaeological excavations. Archaeological excavation is controlled documented destruction.

In *The Last Crusade*, Professor Jones defines *archaeology* as the search for facts (as opposed to truth) about the past, thereby recognizing the interpretive, conditional nature of our knowledge. He further notes that most archaeology is done in the library, not the field. This view may not be far from the reality of the situation today, but library (or even laboratory) research is not the way most people, including archaeologists, would characterize the discipline.

*Archaeology* is the study of (mainly) past human behavior through the examination of the physical byproducts of that behavior. True, archaeology includes ethnoarchaeology and modern material culture studies, both of which involve contemporary peoples, but the discipline is defined by its access to the past. The main contribution of archaeology to the social sciences is its ability to define and analyze long-term changes in human behavior and adaptation to changing environments. Archaeology provides time depth to our understanding of the human condition beyond what can be attained from the study of historical records.

If one envisions archaeological deposits as three-dimensional archives, horizontal movement across the surface represents change in location, or the spatial dimension. Vertical movement through the archive involves the temporal dimension. To go back in time, we go down through soil layers, and we do it with archaeological excavation. Excavation is the means by which we access the past, the most basic, defining aspect of archaeology. Unfortunately, archaeological sites are finite, nonrenewable resources. Once disturbed, they cannot be replaced or restored to their original condition.

Running a bulldozer through a site to build a building or highway is destructive, but archaeological excavation is, in a sense, just as destructive. Although digging a site takes longer with shovels, trowels, and paintbrushes than with a bulldozer or backhoe, the end result is similar: The archaeological deposits are gone forever. Archaeology is one of the few scientific disciplines in which the research methods destroy the objects of our study. As a result, we have an important responsibility to justify our excavation activities and to use state-of-the-art techniques.

Because archaeological destruction proceeds more slowly and methodically than looting or construction disturbances, it is possible to make detailed records of artifacts and features before their depositional contexts are destroyed. This recording process is an absolute requirement in archaeology, distinguishing our work from the actions of others who dig in sites and to some extent justifying the consumption of our archaeological resources. However, it is not possible to record every potential observation or piece of information that could be obtained from an archaeological site. The choices of what to record and what not to record are (or should be) made in response to the questions we seek to answer; there are no data except in response to questions.

## JUSTIFYING THE DESTRUCTION

Destruction of a site through archaeological excavation is justifiable if the work is done responsibly and ethically. We must make defensible choices about where to excavate, how to recover the data, and how to report our research. In addition, we must take care to protect the site during excavation, to ensure that the useful data are actually recovered and not destroyed by the elements while they are exposed.

In other words, the careful destruction of archaeological sites can be justified when it is the result of an appropriate research design. Or can it? Can contemporary archaeology be characterized as research? Some archaeologists have suggested that archaeology conducted in the service of CRM is not research at all (Dunnell 1984:67–68; Patterson 1978:134). If one accepts this view, the implication is that contemporary archaeology (which is mostly CRM) is not research oriented and, therefore, cannot be used to justify the destruction inherent in archaeological excavation. Is this position tenable?

Dunnell (1984) describes archaeological research as a process that begins with a problem or a research question to be answered. The researcher then chooses the location where excavations will be undertaken to answer the question and the methods that will be used to obtain the necessary data. It is emphasized that the archaeologist makes the *choice* of research methods and areas in response to the research problem. Dunnell argues that CRM archaeology does not follow this research model because most archaeologists do not have a choice about where they work:

> The generation of a CRM project has nothing whatsoever to do with an archaeological problem. CRM is generated by nonarchaeologists and concerns potential impact on a particular piece of real estate. The initial input is spatial. . . . The notion of relevance that guides the selection of resources in problem-oriented research is replaced by a less well-defined notion of significance. (68)

This viewpoint, intended to emphasize a dichotomy between academic and CRM archaeology, can be challenged on at least three grounds. (1) Archaeology is not the only discipline that must operate in the context of externally generated restrictions and demands. In spite of strictures on research design, scientists in other disciplines have somehow managed to conduct research. (2) Archaeology has been coping with external constraints for some time. One cannot choose to excavate a site where the landowner has not given permission for access, even if it is the "key" site necessary for answering the most important research question in the region. One cannot choose to excavate sites in a foreign country without obtaining the necessary permits from the host country. One cannot import soil samples from foreign countries for laboratory analyses without submitting to strict U.S. Customs controls on processing and disposal methods. Moreover, funding constraints have been endemic in archaeology for a long time; rarely, if ever, does a researcher have the financial resources to pursue whatever studies he might choose. Even (or perhaps especially) in the world of non-CRM archaeology, researchers have had to design their studies with funding constraints in mind. (3) Dunnell's view seems to reflect inflexibility in the use of problem-solving strategies (Adams 1986:71). Overreliance on a single, traditional approach may create unnecessary impediments to research:

> Just as we use physical tools for physical tasks, we employ conceptual tools for conceptual tasks. To familiarize yourself with a tool, you may experiment with it, test it in different situations, and evaluate its usefulness. The same method can be applied to conceptual tools. Our ability as thinkers is dependent on our range and skill with our own tools. (Adams 1986:76)

Making the best use of archaeological sites that must be consumed can be challenging, but the research opportunities provided by contemporary CRM cannot be overlooked. It is well known that the earliest investigations in many parts of the world focused on the largest and most obvious sites or those closest to major access routes. One of the main advantages of CRM work is that researchers are sometimes forced to investigate areas and sites that would have been overlooked in the past (see sidebar 3.1 and Toolkit, volume 1).

In fact, with much of today's archaeological research focusing on regional settlement pattern characteristics, small sites may even be more important than large ones, because they represent newly identified components of settlement systems (Schiffer and Gummerman 1977:242). They are also potentially more easily interpretable because their contents may be less complex than at a larger site with many overlapping occupations (Binford 1982).

It is true that project area boundaries are often oddly shaped, but even this can be used to advantage. Pipeline corridors that are several hundred miles long can be conceived of as transects to sample site

### 3.1.  THE KEYSTONE SITE

The Keystone site (41EP493) , the earliest pithouse village in the western United States, dating back at least 4,500 years, was discovered through CRM (O'Laughlin 1980), as was 41EP492, an unusually late pithouse occupation dating to the "pueblo period" (Carmichael 1985). Both sites (figures 3.1 and 3.2) were discovered in an area of El Paso where construction disturbances related to the Keystone Dam flood control project were anticipated but that had not been examined during previous research in the region. The first evidence of a burned ramada ever identified in the El Paso region (figure 3.3) was discovered at 41EP751, a small site impacted by pipeline construction near the eastern edge of the U.S. Army Air Defense Center, Fort Bliss (New Mexico State University [NMSU] 1989:859–64).

characteristics in various landform settings (Carmichael 1978; NMSU 1989). Individually, a ten-acre well pad study might not contribute much information, but, over a period of years, examination of hundreds of such parcels may generate a useful regional sample for conducting a variety of synthetic and predictive analyses. Even very small-scale excavations can be creatively used to generate useful data sets. Recently, students at the University of Texas at El Paso conducted a small but fruitful research project on materials obtained from test pits excavated where orchard trees were going to be planted within an Archaic campsite on private property (see chapter 5).

Even sites that are partially disturbed or overlain with debris from modern activities may present useful research opportunities (see sidebar 3.2). Disturbance does not automatically relegate a site to an insignificant status. "The failure . . . of any project to yield research results reflects less upon the characteristics of the resources than upon the competence, background, and interests of the investigators" (King and Hickman 1973:366).

Perhaps CRM archaeology projects don't always meet contemporary research ideals, but they can and should (and the same could be said for archaeology generally). Freedom of choice does not define research; how one investigates observed patterns in the archaeological

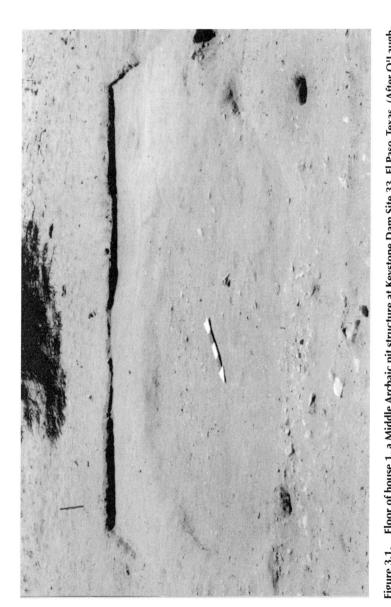

Figure 3.1.   Floor of house 1, a Middle Archaic pit structure at Keystone Dam Site 33, El Paso, Texas. (After O'Laughlin 1980, courtesy U.S. Army Corps of Engineers.)

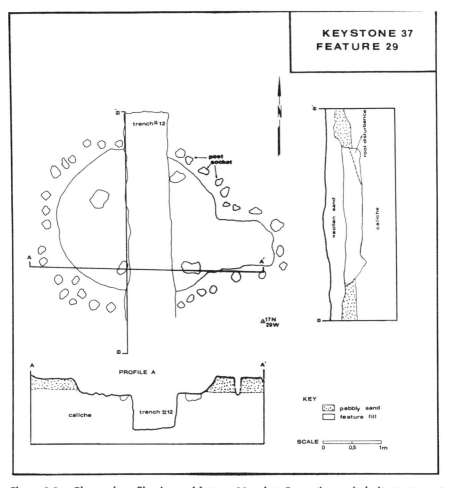

Figure 3.2.   Plan and profile views of feature 29, a late Formative period pit structure at Keystone Dam Site 37, El Paso, Texas.  (After Carmichael 1985, courtesy U.S. Army Corps of Engineers.)

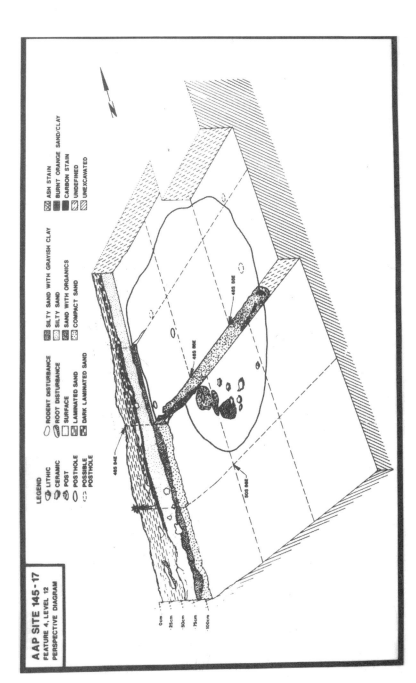

**Figure 3.3.** Stratigraphic block diagram of a prehistoric ramada structure (showing support posts and burned roof elements, but lacking walls), AAP Site 145–17, Fort Bliss, Texas. (After New Mexico State University 1989; courtesy U.S. Bureau of Land Management, California Desert District.)

## 3.2.  THE FILLMORE PASS SITE (FB-1613)

FB-1613 is a complex multicomponent lithic site located near the Texas–New Mexico border on Fort Bliss. The site contains evidence of Paleoindian, Archaic, and early Formative occupations, and most of the assemblage is probably assignable to the preceramic periods. Excavations yielded the largest collection of Folsom artifacts in the region, including some two dozen Folsom points and preforms, more than sixty channel flakes, and hundreds of scrapers. Unfortunately, the deposits were shallow, and the cultural materials from different time periods overlapped. The original research design called for developing and testing techniques that might be used to spatially separate the partially overlapping assemblages from different time periods (Stiger 1986). The field methods included the standard practice of recording artifact location with point proveniencing or within 1 × 1–meter units, in order to describe any spatial patterning. It is necessary to determine whether patterns differ significantly from random or background distributions (Kellog 1987). How could this be done?

Like many places on Fort Bliss, the area around FB-1613 was once part of the impact area for an artillery firing range. As a result, shrapnel from exploded shells is scattered throughout the site. In the research design, the shrapnel distribution was defined as an independent control on the degree of disturbance to assist in the recognition and description of artifact patterning.

record does. Charles Darwin did not choose to visit the Galapagos Islands, nor did he make plans in advance to study variation in finches. He made good use of the opportunities presented to him. Archaeologists should be prepared to do the same.

Twenty-six years ago, Schiffer and Gummerman (1977:130) remarked, "Hopefully, it will not be necessary much longer to justify the development of explicit research designs in archaeology." Unfortunately, it is still necessary. Recently, a colleague reviewed a research design for archaeological work to be conducted in southeastern New Mexico. When the agency representative was asked what specific research questions would be addressed through hypothesis testing, the gist of the response was "Ten years ago we used to do hypothesis testing, but not anymore. It's better to just ask a general question, like whether or not there is any biface reduction technology. We'll be using quarter-inch mesh screen to look for it." Unless one specifies how biface reduction technology will be recognized and how the evidence will be recovered, it seems this project will be a hit-or-miss undertaking. Screening of this sort is likely to miss the evidence for biface reduction technology anyway, as well as whole classes of low-visibility sites such as Apache camps.

Research designs are necessary to ensure that a site's irreplaceable potential to advance knowledge is not squandered (Raab 1984:55). The scientific importance (and National Register eligibility under criterion D) of a site is determined by its research potential:

> In order to determine the significance of a site, enough testing must be done to establish the nature of the potential information that will answer research questions found in the State Plan or any other research documentation outlined in the research proposal. The fact that there are undisturbed deposits of cultural material beneath the plow zone is not in itself enough to say the site is significant. (Davis 1982:B-10)

Today, several states have plans for archaeological conservation that outline archaeological knowledge in each region of the state. The best plans (e.g., Davis 1982) are useful outlines of the research needed in a particular region, at the time they were written. While these state plans may be useful in providing "boilerplate" questions in assessing significance and structuring research questions, they are rarely up-to-date, so it is incumbent upon the archaeologist to be knowledgeable about the current state of research.

Research potential can change in relation to new research questions, new technological capabilities, or the near-threshold of data redundancy for certain resource types. To be current, one must attend conferences and read the journals. A lithic scatter lacking diagnostic projectile points might be written off as having negligible research value. But if the debitage includes many obsidian flakes, the site may have enormous potential to yield information, through chemical sourcing analysis and hydration dating, on population movements and chronology. Therefore, research designs need to be dynamic documents, not boilerplate introductory sections in a project report. It is not only acceptable but necessary to examine sites using new, creative, even experimental technologies. If we routinely avoid doing so, we will fail to define the real research potential of sites, fail to serve our client's compliance needs, fail to address archaeology's conservation ethic, and fail to advance archaeological research.

[A] little reflection will reveal that the successful research design is an outgrowth of the creative application of archaeological expertise to the problem at hand. This endeavor requires on the part of the investigator nothing less than an exhaustive knowledge of archaeological method and theory, a close familiarity with previous research on the problem, and an intimate acquaintance with available information on the archaeological resources. (Schiffer and Gummerman 1977:130)

If a single individual does not command all these areas of expertise, preparation of the research design should be a group undertaking. If you or the staff of your research facility or contracting firm lacks expertise in a particular region or analytical technique, team with or subcontract to the experts. See Toolkit, volume 1, for more details on developing research designs.

## EXCAVATION AND THE CONSERVATION ETHIC

Some people believe that archaeologists want to excavate all the sites they find, but this is not generally true. Most contemporary archaeologists work within a conservation ethic, and those who don't, should. We would rather see a site preserved for future excavation, when techniques will be more advanced.

Although the boundaries of our study areas are often determined by external considerations, archaeologists do have a considerable amount of choice about where to excavate. Plog (1984:91–93) outlines a series of questions to consider before we can justify our decisions about which sites to excavate and how much to excavate. Is the site important for its potential to help answer an important research question? Excavating a site merely to train students to dig is not acceptable. The most effective investigations will be those that are directed toward answering specific questions and those that consider carefully how much excavation is required to meet the research goals. Out of economic considerations, we rarely excavate an entire site, and it is usually good practice to sample site deposits for other reasons, too, such as avoiding data redundancy, minimizing curation costs, and preserving part of the site for later researchers.

Can the research question be answered using an existing database? Museums collections are curated ostensibly so they are available to researchers in perpetuity. Often they have received minimal analysis. There may be provenience problems with museum collections, and they may have been collected using less refined techniques than would be the case today, but existing collections are underutilized (see Toolkit, volume 6). If a research question can be answered with a museum collection, unnecessary excavation can be avoided.

If you have a choice, it is better to excavate sites that are less well protected and more susceptible to looting, vandalism, or erosion damage. For this reason, it often makes sense to excavate sites on private lands, where sites have fewer legal protections. It may also be possible to obtain some kinds of data from partially disturbed sites, allowing for the conservation of better-preserved examples. While conducting research at the University of Illinois, Robert Clouse excavated portions of an upland Paleoindian site, a rare find in east-central Illinois. Although the site was in an agricultural field, it was discovered after only one pass of the plow, and Clouse was able to excavate the undisturbed ridges between the new furrows, obtaining the data he needed and leaving the unplowed portion of the site intact.

Finally, we should consider conducting excavations at sites with good potential for public interpretation. Good potential could be indicated by ease of access, proximity to other public facilities and attractions, or a location where features and the archaeological research activities can be readily observed. Such excavations are responsive to the public interest in archaeology and provide opportunities to educate visitors about the conservation ethic and proper research methods.

## CONTROLLING THE DESTRUCTION

As we saw in chapter 2, excavation techniques have changed considerably in the past two centuries. It is possible to point plot every artifact, but for many research questions, such precision is not necessary. The appropriate level of precision depends on the research questions and the nature of the site. For example, at the Erbie site (Lafferty et al. 1988), the research design called for statistical sampling using 50 × 50–centimeter control columns, and then opening several 2 × 2–meter units. About a third of the way through the control column excavations, it became apparent that the site was much smaller than previously thought. In addition, a Mississippian period house, which had never been excavated in the Arkansas Ozarks, was discovered. The focus of the excavation was redirected toward the house feature, and the precision of the control was increased to one meter. If you are looking for activity areas that are two to three meters in diameter, then you must use smaller units. If you are trying to find pit features in an apparently homogeneous midden, then smaller units are called for.

Extensive documentation of the work on a site is very important. Detailed field notes are crucial. Photographs, including color slides, black-and-white prints, and digital images of the general site, taken before, during, and after excavations, are important. All excavations should be documented with detailed maps, notes, profiles, plan view drawings, detailed photographs of features, and logs to keep track of all recovered finds and samples.

It is important to take samples that you might not plan to use. Soil columns and flotation columns may prove useful for answering unanticipated questions in the future. Soil samples should be reserved from all features and burials. We recommend floating total contents of all excavated features to recover low-frequency seeds and other materials.

Be flexible but thorough. When the inevitable unanticipated discovery happens, modify your research plan to accommodate it. If you are excavating a stratified deposit and interested in the early levels, you should also properly excavate the upper levels. These deposits may hold the key to why that site was important in the earlier times. At some significant sites in the East, the upper levels were bulldozed to get at the earlier levels. The investigators later regretted doing this, but by then nothing could be done about it.

Excavation areas should be protected from the elements. Usually, plastic sheeting over the excavations will lessen damage from rain or wind and can help secure the site from the curious when excavations are not in progress.

## SITE SECURITY

Site security precautions are situation-dependent. A good precaution, as well as a general safety requirement of the Occupational Safety and Health Administration (OSHA), is to put orange barrier fencing around the excavations to keep the unwary from falling into the pits. The fencing also lets the public know that they should not be inside the fence. Appropriate "Keep Out—No Trespassing" signs are also a good idea. On federal and Indian lands, a warning of ARPA violations might be appropriate. If livestock are nearby, electric fencing might prove necessary.

When conducting a large excavation, it is good to keep a low profile with the press. Eventually, the press will find out that something is going on, and we owe the public an account of our work, so plan to give a press conference or interviews at the end of the project when there is something to show. Journalists have ethics, too, and in the case of an ongoing project, they will usually understand the need to protect the site. When you do a press conference or interview, plan what your main points are going to be. See Toolkit, volume 7, for details on media relations.

Some regions entail severe threats to sites from looters and vandals. Many places have long traditions of pothunting. Pothunters have become nocturnal, especially since the passage of NAGPRA. Farmers tell of tractors dropping into four-foot-deep holes dug by looters in one night. In such situations, it is necessary to hire a security service to guard the site at night and during weekends. If the guards do not show up, one of your crew members might have to stay on the site. Provide a cell phone and lots of coffee, but tell your crew person to get out of the way quickly if she thinks she is in danger.

Vandalism is a significant problem in the western United States, especially in remote areas, on public lands, and on open lands adjacent to populated areas. One of us (D.L.C.) has experienced vandalism that seemed to be the result of frustration over new development. Apparently mistaking our grid stakes for the construction boundaries, the site's neighbors routinely removed our grid corners and datum stakes in the evenings or over the weekends. At another site, we have experienced persistent vehicular vandalism, as the local weekend warriors seemed to think that our excavation units presented a great opportunity to test their vehicles' suspensions. Despite the presence of locked fences and barriers (which were themselves vandalized and removed), trucks were purposely driven through prehistoric pithouses and storage pits.

Even the presence of military police and guards is not always effective. Lining units with plastic and backfilling each night is time-consuming but helpful. We also routinely establish a whole series of datum offsets, which are rebar stakes or steel pipes set back from several of the datum points on our grid line, hidden in the brush, or at least out of the off-road vehicle traffic area, and pounded flush with the ground surface. Then, whenever the grid is disturbed, the task of reestablishing control of the site is simplified.

## TRUTH IN REPORTING

Truthfulness in reporting the facts of our research is an ethical responsibility that should be understood by all professional archaeologists. It should not be necessary to remind researchers to tell the truth. Sadly, experience suggests that veracity in reporting research results is not always the highest priority.

Some years ago, one of us (D.L.C.) conducted a well pad survey in the Gypsum Plain region, an area of gypsum karst topography in southeastern New Mexico (Carmichael 1985). The client was a mining company, and during the first day in the field, I was accompanied by one of the staff geologists. After examining perhaps half a dozen well pads, the annoyed geologist asked what I was doing—what was I looking at on the ground, and why was I taking so many notes? Why was I taking so long at each well pad? When I informed him that I had discovered prehistoric sites at half the well pads and that I was recording them according to standard archaeological field procedures, he was shocked and apologetic. He told me that the archaeological contractor his company usually hired had never found anything on any of the surveys they conducted in this area. He said, "They just drive to the well pad, get out and walk around the truck, announce that there's nothing here, and charge us $100!" Clearly, the other contractor wasn't truthfully reporting the actual field conditions, exposing his client to a possible public relations disaster, and, just as clearly, the client had a very unfortunate conception of what archaeologists do and how they do it.

This is not an isolated case. Consider the contract archaeology firm in Wyoming whose main clients are companies in the oil and gas industry. The firm printed up nice trifold brochures announcing their company motto: "We strive to prevent any client downtime!" They accomplish this goal, in part, by conducting "clearance surveys" of well pads and access roads by riding as passengers atop the earth-moving equipment and reporting that no cultural resources were observed. Oh, and did they forget to mention the eight inches of snow on the ground at the time of the survey?

A colleague working in New Mexico reported a different sort of veracity problem that occurred on a federal contract. Data recovery excavations were undertaken on a lithic and ceramic scatter that had been assigned to the late Formative prior to the start of excavation. During laboratory analysis of the artifact collections, the lithic

technology specialist identified several Archaic (7500–2000 B.P.) projectile points and three channel flakes, the very distinctive debitage
resulting from the manufacture of Folsom fluted points ten thousand years old. Artifact analysis clearly indicated the presence of Paleoindian (often around ten thousand years or older) and Archaic
components, but the project director refused to accept this evidence.
A preliminary report had already been submitted, and the project director argued that the client had already fulfilled its Section 106 responsibilities. The internal dispute over what data should be
reported was eventually resolved at the level of the State Historic
Preservation Office; the artifact analysis was included as an appendix, and both interpretations of the site were presented in a revised
final report. Whatever the reason for submitting a report before the
analysis was completed, the whole episode never would have happened had the project director simply reported the actual research
findings. At least other researchers now have the benefit of the data
should they choose to reevaluate the report authors' findings. Such
is not always the case.

An archaeologist working near San Antonio, Texas, contacted one
of us (D.L.C.) with questions about the identification of Apache sites.
Test excavations in a burned rock midden believed to be late Archaic
in age yielded a radiocarbon date of 140 ±60 B.P. There was no reason
to suspect contamination or intrusive modern charcoal, and the researcher was understandably excited about the possibility of reporting the rare find of a protohistoric or historic Apache camp. However,
the researcher's suggestion of a possible Apache affiliation was met
with great resistance by most of his colleagues and his boss. The idea
that the site might be attributable to the Apaches was overruled because it didn't fit the expectation that it should contain artifacts of
Euro-American origin. As a result, the site was reported as being a disturbed Late Archaic site, with the late (i.e., "intrusive") radiocarbon
date being the basis for inferring disturbance. Is it any wonder that
Apache sites are so rare in the archaeological database, when we are
so quick to assign them to the Archaic period?

Apaches were present in much of New Mexico and Texas for several hundred years; they must have left thousands of campsites behind, but very few have been documented. We are probably not
recognizing them because they resemble other sorts of sites, and as
long as we continue to dismiss late radiocarbon dates and other evidence because they don't fit our expectations, we will continue to be
fooled by the data we create. Perhaps most distressing, if we don't at

least report the "intrusive" date and fairly discuss the possibility of an Apache affiliation, it will be very difficult for researchers interested in that particular issue to locate and reevaluate the data relevant to their research interests. We are building a database for our colleagues, not just running a business.

These examples exhibit several different sorts of misrepresentation, ranging from personal biases, to procedural corner cutting, to probable fraud. Such "untruths" impede our efforts to build a reliable database and to share useful knowledge within our profession and with our sponsors and with the public. Veracity is a key component of our ethical responsibilities to our colleagues, our clients, and the public. Misrepresentation, lying, and fraud are not to be tolerated in this profession. Frauds waste time and effort, and once discovered, the perpetrators' data can no longer be trusted and are forever suspect. In archaeology, information about an artifact or its associations in the ground is ultimately based on the word of the archaeologist. As a profession, we must be totally intolerant of liars; veracity exists at the heart of the Register of Professional Archaeologists' code of conduct. Misrepresentation of research results can ruin a reputation, result in the loss of a job or career, and undermine the public's trust in the archaeological profession generally.

## CONSULTATION WITH AFFECTED GROUPS

Ethical guidelines for professional archaeologists have been prepared by several professional associations, including the Society for American Archaeology, and the Register of Professional Archaeologists (see Smith and Burke 2003). All such archaeological guidelines identify our responsibility to care for the archaeological database as one of our highest ethical priorities. This is as it should be. However, we should not forget that as archaeologists we are also anthropologists, and, as such, we should be responsive to the professional ethical guidelines established for anthropologists as a whole.

Among the principles of professional ethics articulated by the American Anthropological Association, the highest priority is our responsibility to protect the interests of those people we study or those who are most affected by our research. For archaeologists working in the United States, the people affected by our research will often be Native Americans. It is an ethical responsibility, now required by law (NAGPRA), to consult with Native Americans (and others) who may be affected by our excavation projects. While working under contract to the U.S. Air Force, one of us (D.L.C.) directed consultation activities involving some forty tribal groups in fifteen states. A workable set of procedures was developed that have since been formalized as the Air Force guidelines for consultation with Native American groups in the context of land use planning. While these guidelines do not constitute a "cookbook" for consultation, they have been used in developing other agency guidelines, and they provide a useful starting point for designing culturally appropriate consultations. Stapp and Burney (2002) provide an excellent recent source on consultation with American Indian tribes.

No one can reasonably dispute the complex nature of today's archaeology. We must deal with colleagues and publics, we must work with an increasingly complex science, and we must be ethically true to ourselves, our colleagues, and those with whom we work. In chapter 4, we will see how some of these matters play out in our actual fieldwork as we identify, characterize, and test sites. We are now moving into the "down and dirty" parts of archaeology, but remembering the higher and perhaps more noble concerns of what we do remains important. Try to remember these as we move through the next chapters.

Ethical guidelines relating to the conduct of archaeology and interaction with Native Americans may be found at the following websites:

| | |
|---|---|
| Society of American Archaeology | www.saa.org/aboutSAA/Ethics |
| American Anthropological Association | www.aaanet.org/committees/ethics |
| Register of Professional Archaeologists | www.rpanet.org |
| U.S. Air Force, AFI32-7065 | www.epublishing.af.mil/pubfiles/af/32/afi32-7065/ |

# 4

# SITE TESTING, EXCAVATION, AND CHARACTERIZATION

The harder you look, the more you find.

*—Anonymous*

By now, you know that excavation should recover artifacts and data to address important research questions. You know, too, that as an excavator you are answerable to several stakeholders. Yet all of our discussion in the last chapter doesn't address the nitty-gritty of actual field practice. As we move toward actual excavation, we become interested in identifying, excavating, and describing the range of features at a site and documenting the artifacts associated with them. These general goals present a dilemma, however. Features that are exposed on the ground surface, and therefore observable during surveys, are likely to be more disturbed and have less research potential than intact, buried features. But the buried features are not visible at the surface, so, as people always ask, "How do you know where to dig?"

## HOW DO WE KNOW WHERE TO DIG?

Most archaeologists probably have heard at least one story about the important house or burial or storage pit that was discovered near the end of an excavation project. Sometimes this does indeed happen, but wouldn't we rather use more of our field time excavating features than looking for them? A variety of techniques, some low-tech and some high-tech, can help locate features and otherwise characterize sites. When these techniques are built into a well-conceived research strategy, the results can be remarkably informative.

Geophysical survey and remote sensing often can help you detect features and characterize the subsurface nature of a site prior to excavation. These methods are discussed in volume 2 of the Archaeologist's Toolkit series. Here, we focus on the test excavation techniques commonly used to assess sites prior to large-scale excavation. These techniques also may be used to help develop preservation plans, mitigation plans, and National Register documentation and for other purposes that require more knowledge about the site than is typically obtained during the survey phase.

Traditional testing and excavation methods use units such as shovel tests, auger holes, 1 × 1–meter units, 2 × 2–meter units, and hand-excavated trenches. For most CRM projects, it is best to begin with the quicker, less expensive techniques, such as shovel testing, to determine where to place the larger units. Shovel tests and auger holes distributed systematically across a site can help characterize basic elements of the site (e.g., artifact types, feature distribution, and soil types). Larger excavation units can give more detailed data on artifact density and range of feature types.

As Black and Jolly say in volume 1 of the Archaeologist's Toolkit series, "think before you dig," and design your test excavation strategy carefully so you meet your project goals. Figuring out a useful approach is not always easy. Some states have survey standards that require testing at regular intervals, which limits your strategic choices. Scopes of work for a CRM project may make demands for limited samples, usually a percentage of an area of potential effect (APE). Many advocate using random sampling methods to determine placement of test units, while others advocate a stratified random sample wherein a sample is drawn from each of several predetermined units, these based on such attributes as elevation, distance to water or other resources, soils, and vegetative cover. Where sites have already been located, similar approaches can be used. Grid units can be randomly selected for excavation, and they can also be stratified based on some characteristic, often density of surface materials of certain types. Where sampling is random or stratified random, the sample represents the area of survey or the site (see Orton 2000 for a thorough discussion). Many archaeologists forego this more rigorous scientific approach in favor of an intuitive approach based on their prior knowledge of an area. Whatever the choice, methods should be dictated by a justifiable research design.

## TYPES OF TEST AND EXCAVATION UNITS

*Shovel testing* employs a small unit, usually a 30 × 30– to 50 × 50–centimeter square. It is good to standardize the size, so that comparative volumetric data can be computed. During excavation, take notes on the soil description, artifacts present, and depth of each excavation level. Lafferty likes to use a form that has four columns with depths shown on a scale on which excavation levels, field serial numbers, and soil descriptions are recorded. A drawing is completed for each unit, standardizing record keeping. Depths of each excavation level should be measured as excavations are in progress, and the contents should be screened to ensure consistent recovery.

*Auger testing* involves using a three- to fifteen-centimeter diameter auger or posthole digger that can either be hand or machine powered. Although smaller in diameter, auger holes can extend much deeper than shovel tests that seldom penetrate more than fifty to seventy centimeters. The smaller size of auger holes and problems of compaction make it essential to describe, measure, and segregate the different soil layers as they are being excavated. Each defined or auger bucketful should be screened. If you are using a machine-powered auger with screeners following behind, each stratum needs to be laid aside separately and labeled so the records coincide. A third crew member should describe the profile and record provenience data. The person making the description should fill out the provenience tag and leave it with each unit to be screened.

*Large-scale units* are traditionally 1 × 1 meter, 2 × 2 meters, or larger units. They provide a broader three-dimensional view of the deposits and can show the plan view and cross-sections of features and soil horizons. The orientation of the unit should always be recorded on the site map. The unit's orientation is very much dependent on the site. Generally, orientation to magnetic north makes sense, particularly if magnetometer work is anticipated. Often it makes more sense to orient the grid with the topography, such as a terrace, the opening of a bluff-edge rock shelter, or the alignment of structures visible on the surface of the site. Units can be combined end to end, to create trenches, or expanded out in several directions to provide a broad, horizontal exposure to explore activity area patterning. Some archaeologists favor these for testing where they are economically feasible because they allow the extent of features to be seen more readily than in a small unit where one can often only detect the presence or absence of artifacts.

The larger the unit, the deeper it is possible to dig but the more time it takes. For example, 1 × 1–meter units are difficult to excavate more than sixty centimeters deep with a long-handled shovel. A 2 × 2–meter unit can easily be extended to the OSHA maximum of four feet for unshored excavations, although units approaching this depth can be dangerous in unstable situations, as when sand occurs beneath fine-grained sediments. (See sidebar 4.1 for more details on excavation methods and tools.)

### 4.1. RESOURCES FOR EXCAVATION METHODS, TOOLS, AND SOURCES FOR SPECIALIZED TESTS

Archaeology is no longer a simple field where a shovel, trowel, screen, and a couple of tapes suffice for equipment. You have to consider a wide range of variables every time you head to the field ranging from safety requirements to specialized tests. Appendix 1 lists some of the tools you might wish to consider taking with you and sources for them. The appendix also lists places that do specialized tests from radiocarbon dating to obsidian hydration. Appendix 2 provides mathematical resources you might need in the field and lab from conversion tables for measurements to places to find or generate random number tables to use for excavation unit placement.

No single approach to excavation works for all sites, although some standard approaches need only minor modification for each site. So much depends on research design, contract scopes of work, budgets, and time. We cannot cover all bases here but would like to recommend a few current and out-of-print books, commenting briefly on each. Each provides details on excavation methods and techniques you may find useful. We have taught field schools at different times using Dancey, Hester et al., Joukowsky, and Roskams. All are clearly written, and the Hester et al., Joukowsky, and Roskams books are comprehensive.

Barker, Philip, 2nd ed., rev. and expanded.
  1983   *Techniques of Archaeological Excavation.* New York: Universe.
         Some regard this as the British standard for excavation.
Dancey, William
  1987   *Archaeological Field Methods: An Introduction.* Minneapolis: Burgess.
         This thin volume is a no-nonsense introduction to basic methods.

Drewitt, Peter L.
   1999   *Field Archaeology: An Introduction*. London: Routledge.
          A useful volume whose strength is that it presents excavation as the center-
          piece of a process, starting with planning and moving through publication.
          The emphasis is British, but much applies to all archaeology.

Hester, Thomas R., Harry J. Shafer, and Kenneth L. Feder
   1997   *Field Methods in Archaeology*; 7th ed. Mountain View, Calif.: Mayfield.
          This hefty (nearly six hundred pages) volume is the standard field methods text
          in North America for good reason. It is complete, with a look at variations be-
          tween Classical, Prehistoric, Historical, Nautical, and Industrial Archaeology,
          with part of one chapter on CRM.

Joukowsky, Martha J.
   1980.  *A Complete Manual of Field Archaeology: Tools and Techniques of
          Field Work for Archaeologists*. Englewood Cliffs, NJ: Prentice Hall.
          Now out of print, this compendium provides a wealth of detail. The emphasis
          is on Classical archaeology and large-site excavation, but the techniques are
          well explained.

Roskams, Steve
   2001   *Excavation*. Cambridge: Cambridge University Press.
          Primarily from a British perspective with British examples, the strength of this
          book is that it moves from details about planning to a discussion about
          prospects for the future. Also good is its presentation of material on a wide
          range of site types.

Setting up a unit without a grid is straightforward once the orientation has been decided. Place two pins or stakes the designated distance (one or two meters) apart in the selected orientation. Pull the
hypotenuse (1.4142 or 2.8284 meters) and other leg to the triangle to
set the third and fourth corners (see appendix 2). String the unit, and
you are ready to proceed.

There are at least four different ways to string a unit (figure 4.1).
The most traditional method incorporates a square five- to ten-
centimeter baulk around the stake. Gutter spikes or large nails can be
angled into the corner, or the corner can be cut at a forty-five-degree
angle to provide enough strength to hold the nail. In sands and poorly
consolidated deposits, you can use two pins per corner, set ten centimeters or more back from the edge of the unit in line with each adjacent profile.

Excavation level thickness can be arbitrary or according to stratigraphic level. In most areas, standard arbitrary levels are no thicker

# Excavation Techniques

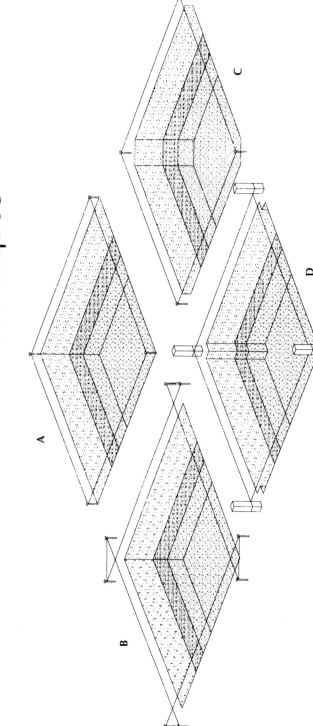

**Figure 4.1.** Different ways of stringing units. *A*, Gutter spikes angled into corners works under heavy soil conditions, such as clay; *B*, triangular off-set is useful when the matrix is unstable such as sand; *C*, triangular baulk around stake; *D*, traditional square stake baulk.

than ten centimeters. Whatever levels are used, always note the top and bottom depths for volumetric control. If the surface is sloping and you are digging in horizontal levels, it is useful to record the depth below the surface of each corner of the unit. Under most soil conditions, the site matrix is passed through 6.25-millimeter (1/4-inch) mesh, 1/8-inch mesh, or window screen. Depending on your research design, it may be advisable to retain some of the fill from each level for water screening, to recover small artifacts (see chapter 5). If the soil is so clayey that it is difficult or impossible to screen, excavation can proceed by thin shovel scraping (or thin cutting), recovering the artifacts as they are encountered or after mapping them in situ. Indicate the method you use on your forms and in your field notes.

Generally, we use a separate level form for each level of each excavation unit. The form includes spaces for the excavators' names, date of the excavation, site number, unit number, level, depths, field serial numbers of the samples collected in the unit, excavation techniques, observations of soil color and texture, and photograph numbers. Graph paper on the back of the form is used for mapping the plan view of features, point-provenienced (piece-plotted) artifacts (artifacts that are precisely mapped and usually given their own field serial number), and disturbances observed in each level. Once the unit is completed, a drawing is made of one or more profiles. Some unit profiles are all the same, and it is a waste of time to draw more than one. Conversely, we have worked in units that had different features exposed in all four walls, and it was important to record all four profiles.

When testing a site, it is important to excavate into the underlying "sterile" deposits. A minimum of twenty centimeters will usually indicate you have reached sterile deposits, but occasionally it may be necessary to go even deeper. Without excavating below the deepest cultural deposit, you have no assurance that you have found the bottom of the site. Even if auger testing suggests that cultural deposits do not underlie a particular soil horizon, the larger volume excavated by a 1 × 1–unit can help you find deeper, low-density components that may be important. In alluvial settings, try to sink an auger or shovel probe deeper than the bottom of the test unit, just to check for any recognizable components.

When you reach what appears to be the bottom of the deposit or when you decide to bottom out your unit, trowel the profile clean, photograph it, and record the stratigraphy with a scaled drawing. The profile drawing should describe the soil levels in detail and show any features, artifacts, sample locations, inclusions such as burned clay, and postdepositional disturbances (see the later discussion of profiling techniques). When photographing a unit, include a scale, north arrow, and a menu board or chalkboard showing the site number, profile, unit number or grid location, direction, and date. The profile should be evenly lit so that harsh shadows do not detract from the stratigraphic details. Although full sun is acceptable, full shade may provide greater flexibility in the exposure setting. It is often useful to use a canopy, tarp, jacket, box, or crew member to shade the profile and to spray the profile with water from a garden sprayer to enhance color contrasts. Use a digital camera if possible, as well as good-quality outdoor color slide film. If time permits, it may be worthwhile to photograph a profile at different times of the day, when the sunlight strikes it at different angles.

Various coring tools can give you good information on site stratigraphy. Tools range in size from 1.25-centimeter-diameter hand-operated Oakfield corers (which should be standard equipment for all excavation projects) to truck-mounted 7.5-centimeter or larger core rigs. The extracted cores should be tagged and returned to the laboratory. Analyses such as sediment size, organic carbon content, flotation, pollen, radiocarbon, chemical, and many other tests can be conducted on these cores.

Cores should be sealed in polyethylene bags to prevent them from drying out. They should be labeled with their depth range and which end is up in addition to other provenience information. Where multiple cores are taken, the depth range should be measured in the core hole when each segment is pulled. This is because many coarse-grained soils compress in the core. Field notes should describe the samples and depths as they come out of the ground, and each core should be assigned a serial number. For large cores, use heavy-duty boxes to support and protect them. Professional core drillers often provide these as part of their service. (See sidebar 4.2 for more on coring.)

## MECHANICAL EXCAVATION TECHNIQUES

Mechanical excavation techniques, such as backhoe trenching, have been available to archaeologists for many years, but until recently, they were generally looked down upon as a search strategy and used mainly as a last-ditch effort, so to speak. In other words, because of

### 4.2.   CORING

At the Eaker site, coring was designed to determine the depth of cultural deposits. Several cores were placed off-site to determine natural soil conditions. Three three-inch-diameter cores were excavated in segment 8, targeted to three magnetic anomalies. Core 3 was excavated into the same burned house that trench 1 intersected. This core showed a sherd below a burned area and mottling around fifty to sixty centimeters below the surface. It also showed sand to a depth of 160 centimeters below the surface where there is a wedge of silt loam, underlain by sand to a depth of two meters. In contrast, core 1, located twenty-one meters to the west in an area of low magnetic variation, was silt loam to eighty centimeters. A brown sandy loam underlay this deposit. Artifacts were present to 109 centimeters below surface in the core. The cores showed that there were cultural deposits to a depth of more than a meter in some parts of the site.

the destructive potential of mechanical trenching, the backhoe was generally brought in only after the majority of the excavation was completed, just to make sure nothing major was missed before the site was destroyed by construction. However, as archaeologists have followed this strategy over the years, many have learned that some of their most important and unexpected finds have been revealed by backhoe trenching, while other methods have been less fruitful. Furthermore, when subsurface features are discovered early in an excavation, more time can be spent describing and interpreting them, rather than just finding them.

Augers do not penetrate very deeply and do not provide a clear view of the soil strata, and any layering within the auger hole is destroyed as the soil is excavated. In addition to the time saving gained with backhoe trenching, the trenches can be excavated to a greater depth, and the long profiles obtained can reveal features that would not be observed in plan view or in small auger holes or cores. At the Meyer Pithouse Village at Fort Bliss, features were identified by augering, but their identity as pithouses was only revealed through "last-ditch" trenching (Scarborough 1986).

Excavations by the Museum of New Mexico at Luna Village (LA 45507), a pithouse village site in western New Mexico, have convinced researchers of the necessity of mechanical trenching on Mogollon sites. Yvonne Oakes reports that all five of the houses at the site were discovered in backhoe trenches, including (quite unexpectedly) one beneath a gas station and another under an abandoned historic house (Oakes and Zamora 1998). Similar results have been documented on other sites throughout the state.

At the Gobernadora site in El Paso, Myles Miller (1989) compared the rate of feature recovery from the two halves of the same site. The 2 × 2–meter tests previously excavated by Texas Department of Transportation archaeologists contained the same volume of fill as Miller's trenches, but the trenches yielded double the feature recovery.

## TRENCHING AS A STATISTICAL SAMPLING STRATEGY

Trenching provides several advantages in searching for buried features (see also sidebar 4.3). It is more rapid than hand trenching, with obvious attendant cost savings. It also provides relatively easy access to deeply buried deposits. But there is another sort of advantage to trenches, related to the nature of transect sampling.

Transects are effective for identifying features because they only have to catch the edge of a feature in order to identify it. This boundary or edge effect makes transects very efficient sampling units because despite the narrow width of the trench, they sample an area about twice the width of the target feature size. Following the methods outlined by Rice and Plog (1983), backhoe trenching was used as a statistical sampling strategy during the early stages of excavation at site 41EP492 at Keystone Dam in El Paso (Carmichael 1985).

The site grid was laid out in 20 × 20–meter units, which were used as the framework for a systematic sample of transects. A trench was excavated in each 20 × 20–meter unit, alternating along the north-south or east-west centerline. The orientation of the trenches was alternated in order to reduce the chances that they might correspond to some periodicity in the distribution of features and miss them altogether. Calculations predicted that as many as twenty-eight such features might be discovered, and after additional trenching and hand

## 4.3.  BACKHOE TESTING

At Eaker Air Force Base, we were testing sites and finding very deeply buried cultural deposits beneath clean sand. When an excavation unit was stopped because it was thought to have reached sterile sand, standard procedure was to sink a posthole test as deep as possible below the bottom of the test unit. At seven locations, we encountered dense midden deposits at depths of one to two meters below the surface. The ground-penetrating radar profile from 3MS560 showed a thirty-meter-wide depression where we found a midden buried beneath sterile sand. Using a backhoe, we cut sixty meters of trench, and we discovered that a prehistoric sand blow overlay the midden, an earthquake-related feature formed in the liquefaction zone (figure 4.2).

The trench also revealed two thirty-meter wide sand blows atop one another but separated by five centimeters of alluvial clay. In contrast to sand blows recorded on earlier projects, which were formed by the 1811–1812 New Madrid earthquake, these were highly weathered, and prehistoric artifacts occurred above and below the sand blows. By the end of the day, we had found seven more sand blows, five of which appeared to be prehistoric. Because of their association with datable archaeological materials, the sand blows at these sites have become important in dating at least two major periods of prehistoric earthquakes in the New Madrid Seismic Zone.

Figure 4.2.    Backhoe trench 1 at 3MS360 showing the plow zone underlain by the light sand blow. Beneath the sand is intact midden. Flags are in situ artifacts. (Photograph by R. H. Lafferty III.)

excavations, a total of twenty-five were eventually identified. These were pithouses or huts that were very difficult to see in plan view. These were the first examples of such structures discovered in the El Paso region, but now that researchers know how to search for them in trench profiles, they are regularly encountered. Our ability to characterize the site was greatly enhanced by the judicious use of backhoe trenches. The trenches accounted for 50 percent of all the features discovered at the site, and 100 percent of the pithouses.

## MECHANICAL STRIPPING

The use of mechanical stripping is an alternative to hand excavation units when it is desirable to open up a broad, horizontal exposure. Because stripping with a blade or grader is so destructive compared to shovel scraping, the approach is usually used at sites that will be largely destroyed during construction, and even then only after other efforts have been made to recover artifacts. Nevertheless, mechanical stripping can be especially useful for the removal of sterile or disturbed deposits overlying culture-bearing layers. By quickly removing overburden and by opening up large areas at a given level, stripping facilitates the recording of clusters of features.

## RECORDING STRATIGRAPHY

Archaeological sites exist on and in a matrix. Sometimes the matrix is relatively simple, and sometimes it can be complex. Relatively stable surfaces with minimal deposition are at the simple end of the scale, while buildup through alluviation can lead to deeper and more complex deposits. Both the simple and complex matrices may contain evidence of soil formation and of other processes that are critical in archaeological interpretation. Therefore, it is vital to make accurate records of the soils and deposits through which you excavate, regardless of whether your site is in an upland setting, an alluvial fan, a terrace, or a floodplain.

Many natural processes cause sediments to accumulate. Chief among these in much of North America is deposition by rivers, which results in the building of terraces. Alluvial fans build up at the mouths of creeks and rivers. In the arid West, mass wasting of bedrock builds colluvial talus deposits along the bases of hills and mountains. Loess (windblown silt) deposits can be many meters thick, even in uplands. Volcanoes deposit ash over thousands of square kilometers. Earthquakes can eject sand and water over areas as large as ten hectares, as deep as three meters. All of these kinds of deposits often contain archaeological sites.

It is important to record the details of site stratigraphy whether you are working in areas with a relatively stable near-surface soil or a complex depositional history. Where soil horizons or depositional units can be discerned, the excavation should proceed with reference to these by natural strata. The thickness of each stratum (top and bottom depth of each corner) should be recorded so the artifact densities can be calculated. Stratigraphic differences can be identified in the field by a change in soil texture, color, grain size, or compactness. Some of these changes may be depositional, while others may be pedogenic (a result of soil development). When a different stratum is encountered, the unit should be cleaned off to see whether there are features intruding into the underlying stratum.

Careful documentation of intrusions and strata is essential for determining the temporal sequence of samples. Documentation of profiles should be detailed, including complete soil descriptions and point proveniences of any artifacts exposed in the profiles. If you need help with soil descriptions, learn how to identify and describe soil characteristics from a specialist or a manual such as Vogel (2002).

There are several ways of making a scaled drawing of a profile after it is cleaned and all strata of interest are scribed into the wall. One method is to string a line along the length of the profile. The string should be pulled taut and leveled with a line level, carpenter's level, or transit. Large nails, gutter spikes, or surveying pins make good anchors for the string. Draw this level line on your graph paper form. Grid locations should be shown along the top of the drawing. Place a folding engineer's rule or an extended tape parallel to the string. Make sure the tape does not sag, and don't move it until you are done drawing the profile. Using the level line, each point that you want to record can be designated by measuring a certain distance along the line and another distance perpendicular to and above or below the line. A two-person team is best for drawing profiles, one measuring and calling out the points and the other mapping and drawing them. The mapper should be positioned so she is able to see the profile as she draws it, facilitating the inclusion of details. It is most efficient to map the big picture first, starting with the top and bottom of the profile, followed by the major strata and, finally, the features, individual artifacts, and natural disturbances. Instead of making individual measurements perpendicular to your level line, you can also map a profile by stringing the excavation wall with a fifty- or hundred-centimeter grid and overlaying a portable grid with smaller units (such as ten-centimeter squares) over each section as it is mapped.

A detailed site map should be made whenever excavations are undertaken. The map must be scaled and should show the locations of all test units, shovel tests, auger holes, and trenches. Some indication of topography should be shown, preferably using contour lines. Any features such as structures, walls, and depressions should be noted. Water sources and vegetation should be indicated, and prominent trees should be mapped, identified by species, and their diameter measured at chest height. The map should also include anything else that might help future researchers relocate the site and understand what you did. Establishing an unambiguous site datum and depicting it on the map is most important. Scale and north arrow should be included, and the map should be signed and dated.

## CONCLUSION

Archaeologists recognize that the landscapes of the past are often substantially different from those we see today. Geomorphological processes may work to hide the sites created by the people who lived on those landscapes, or they may work to reveal them to us. What we can learn about both the landscapes and the processes can give us some predictive ability to find sites, but mostly locating sites is a matter of technology, ingenuity, and persistence.

Still, what we do when we locate and characterize sites gets us only part way toward understanding the lives of those who created the sites and the cultural processes that influenced them. So far we have looked at dealing with sites at a macro level, but the detail of sites is often in the process of data recovery, the subject of chapter 5.

**5**

# DATA RECOVERY

See the World in a Grain of Sand.

*—William Blake*

Before you start recovering anything, remember that data are not what you are after. Data are indeed the stuff of archaeology— stone, bone and other materials, spatial relationships, and so on—but as soon as you think "Clovis point" (you wish) or even "cortical flake," you are entering the realm of information, the constructs you make in the production of knowledge. Knowledge about the past is the goal, something you hope will resonate throughout the archaeological community when you publish your findings.

The first steps in archaeological knowledge production are theoretical ones. You need to understand first that artifacts and features are not data: They are just artifacts and features. Data are creations you devise based on your research design (see Toolkit, volume 1) and then extract from the artifacts and features. Artifacts and features don't speak for themselves; the archaeologist becomes their "voice." We may like to call what we do "data recovery," but it's worth remembering that it's really "data creation." As you create data, you have to define the scope of the data with which you plan to work.

While we act at a human scale, cultural data resolve at multiple scales, from global to microscopic. You may think of an artifact, for example, as something you can hold in your hand and a landscape as the cultural environment—the background for all those archaeological sites. The problem is that the thing we call a site is an artifact on the landscape, and a projectile point is a landscape, too, a surface

marked by cultural impacts (literally). We are just too big to see a projectile point that way.

So, your first decision about data recovery must refer to the original research design. What are you trying to accomplish? Do you already know the nature of the culture and activity at the site, or is it
still a mystery? Is this basic data recovery, or are you testing specific
hypotheses? Depending on the answer, you may need to be prepared
to "recover" data ranging from the spatial relationships among artifacts and the surrounding environment to pollen grains, the smallest
bits of residue from toolmaking (microdebitage), or chemical residues
from bone decay or foods.

If you fail to appreciate this problem of scale, you may miss data
crucial to an understanding of the phenomena you hope to study.
Consider a simple example: the difference between two sites along a
river, one at a confluence with a creek, and the other downstream
along the bank. If hunters and gatherers saw the former place as more
strategic, because it provided access to two drainages rather than one,
might it have attracted more people over time than the terrace down-
river with only its level well-drained ground to recommend it? If you
bury your nose in a site, you may not even imagine that subtle differences in the site's raw materials, artifacts, and activity areas might
reveal differences of local or regional significance.

## ARTIFACTS AND THINGS

Once you have sorted out your scales of analysis, you can turn to your
data recovery strategy. As noted earlier, as soon as you start naming
things, you are making interpretations, so now is the time and place
to be concerned about classification. The point: You may want to collect "all" the data, but you will retrieve only the data you recognize
from the tiny bit of data that survives.

Much of classification seems to be routine. You may distinguish
material culture objects (artifacts and the residues of production),
natural things used in cultural activity (e.g., hammerstones), and
natural things indirectly affected by cultural activity (e.g., burnt
soil or an unnaturally organic soil stratum). You may expect to find
spatial relationships between and among cultural things. The problem is that you are inevitably imposing your own beliefs, implicitly and explicitly, on material things that do not advertise
themselves at all. If the past speaks, it says what you want to hear!

If you describe a scatter of artifacts as a site, for example, you are assuming a cultural relationship among these things, even though many different individuals, groups, and cultures may have stopped there for many different reasons over time. Because classification is inevitable, the only solution is to think out why you are investigating this particular place and what you hope to gain from the effort.

The issue here is the extent to which you document these artifacts and relations. On an initial reconnaissance survey, for example, you may not need to describe every piece of chert or measure spatial relationships beyond the visible extents of an artifact scatter. If you are excavating, then you will.

## COLLECTION STRATEGY

After thinking about the issues discussed so far, you may worry that no amount of data recovery will ever be enough. Clearly, however, there are limits to what you can do as an archaeologist. The goal is to accomplish what you set out to do; no one expects you to recover a lost world from the meager traces left to us. To resolve this dilemma in a positive way, archaeologists develop collection strategies. What you collect depends on at least two things: what you hope to learn (your research design) and how much data you need to retrieve to learn it. Have you stumbled on the site in a reconnaissance survey? Or is this part of a hypothesis-driven study dealing with some specific archaeological problem? In most excavations, you may need to sort out occupations or activity areas, so you may want to record very carefully in three dimensions exactly where everything is located and collect a representative sample.

You may consider a systematic sampling strategy if you run the risk of being overwhelmed by data—in fact, you probably already use an informal one, if you walk in linear transects across a site. More formalized sampling methods, backed by probability theory, often involve collecting only within predetermined, randomly generated grid squares. This may be particularly effective if you have a comparative problem you want to resolve—say, studying the relative distribution of bison bone types across a meat-processing site so you can speculate on butchering patterns. You may be able to arrive at a satisfactory interpretation informally, but a systematic recovery technique will help eliminate spatial bias that might deform the results.

If you make a mistake in your collection strategy, you are wasting time, perhaps money, and adding to the ever-increasing mountain of useless data. The same caution applies in the lab. Ask yourself this when you are tempted to wave a Munsell chart at a piece of debitage so you can nail down the color: "Does this type of data have any meaning in my analysis?" If the answer is no, give it a basic description and be done with it. The only reason for making collections in the long term is to provide material for someone else to study. Let him do it!

## THE WAYS AND MEANS

Excavation recovers only a tiny fraction of what might have been a habitation, a production site, or other theater of cultural activity. The vagaries of preservation mean that many tools and tool parts made of perishable materials such as plant fibers, wood, leather, and bone may break down quickly under adverse conditions.

### SURFACE RECORDING AND RECOVERY

An artifact exposed on the ground surface is usually not where the maker or user left it. Time is always a culprit, working with wind or water erosion, slope movement, plowing, and other natural and cultural forces. Because you tend to learn most about people, places, and events from the spatial relationships among material things, surface finds will probably not yield as much information as artifacts in situ. Sometimes, however, surface finds might be the only data you have. It is a rare archaeologist who has not found artifacts side by side that are separated by thousands of years. Such mixed assemblages are palimpsests, a word we've adapted from the printing trade to describe artifact assemblages that have become jumbled because either there was no interval of soil deposition between occupations, or the soil that did separate the occupations eroded away.

If this is the situation you face, all is not lost. Temporal and functional diagnostics such as identifiable projectile point or ceramic types, scrapers, or fire-cracked rock can help you build a picture of what happened. You may also be able to map the "horizontal stratigraphy," the spatial distribution of materials across a locality, if the artifacts may have remained more or less in the same place. This is where knowledge of the terrain and the geomorphology are invaluable. You need to be certain that a flood, sheetwash, or slope movement did not transport your artifacts from elsewhere. Finally, do not assume that all the artifacts in an assemblage derived from similar activities. Ponder this question: A toolmaker's debitage may be identical at two different places, but do these scatters offer up the same interpretation if one of the sites is a hunting blind and the other is a staging ground for ceremonial activities?

An important advantage of a surface scatter is the fact that you can map the entire exposed assemblage, if you need to, piece by piece, and therefore quickly define its extent (see Toolkit, volume 2). Careful mapping is key to any subsequent excavation. Of course, cultural material is scattered across the landscape, so what you are really doing is isolating a discrete locus of cultural activity. In a reconnaissance survey, you may find it helpful to stick a pin flag in the ground at every artifact location or, if the finds are too dense, on the outlying edges of a scatter. Pin flags are great because they allow you to see patterning in artifact distribution, but they also call attention to the site. If you are concerned that you are advertising a site location, then use discrete markers.

Once you have surveyed the entire surface, you can map in the artifacts, features, and aspects of the physical setting. If precise spatial relationships are crucial, plot every artifact and feature with a Total Station or theodolite. With very little effort you can generate a computer-aided design (CAD) image from the locational information, giving you a precise map of the area. If you only need to map the general location of artifact clusters or features, a geographic positioning system (GPS) unit is ideal. A unit with real-time differential correction will allow you to map points, lines, and polygons (enclosed shapes) with submeter precision; one without this feature will still get you within several meters, which may be okay for a reconnaissance survey.

When you have finished mapping and taking photographs, you need to invoke your collection policy and get to work. An important point: You may be the last person to see artifacts that you do not collect, especially if you are surveying in a proposed construction area. It is therefore a good idea to have a field identification procedure in place so that you can quickly record some basic data on the artifacts observed (e.g., type of object, material, function, relative size, cultural attribution). You can then pick up the objects you plan to take to the lab for further study.

There is no point in collecting for its own sake. We already know that people have left traces of daily life on the landscape for thousands of years. We do not need any more proof. Having said that, you may want to save something because it is old and uncommon, even though you know it is not going to add significantly to your study. We cannot cling to every element of the past, however, because if we did, we'd have little room to move! Never forget that the traces you find usually relate to someone else's ancestors. The descendants may not just want you to be respectful—they may not want you to interfere in any way at all, despite your legal rights or obligations. Sometimes you simply have to let things go. If you do, don't get upset when collectors move in, pick up what you left, and complain that you "missed" things.


## MOVING DIRT

When you need to explore below the ground surface, you have to resolve the fundamental problem: your lack of X-ray vision! Deciding where to dig takes careful observation and planning. You may have already taken the first step, assuming that the artifacts on the surface reflect the positioning of any below. As this may not be the case, depending on the site taphonomy, the next step is to devise a technique that provides you with a good general impression of the subsurface. If your project area has cutbanks, gullies, rodent burrows, or even anthills, you can learn quite a lot without digging. If you are in an agricultural area, the county soil map will outline the soil characteristics and formation processes. Or you might be fortunate to be in an area that a geomorphologist has already analyzed. If you can, conduct a magnetometer, soil resistivity, GPR, or other geophysical survey. The information you retrieve from these preliminary efforts could lead you from aimless digging for that elusive needle in the haystack to the ground truthing of potential features. At the very least, you should have shovels and a soil corer or auger, so you can explore the subsurface in the traditional way.

The goal of subsurface data recovery is not only to retrieve artifacts but to expose the traces of cultural activity remaining on what were once ground surfaces. Visualization of these buried contexts is very difficult at the best of times. Over the tens, hundreds, or thousands of years separating components, there may have been any number of impacts that added, removed, or otherwise disturbed the deposits. It is therefore extremely advantageous if you can expose a large subsurface area quickly to help inform your subsequent excavations.

At a recent University of South Dakota (USD) Archaeology Laboratory project at Fort Riley, Kansas, for example, we faced the difficult problem of interpreting the cultural resource potential of a large open field and surrounding woods at the confluence of two creeks, an area of more than fifty acres (Molyneaux et al. 2002). To complicate matters, we knew from previous excavations that there were likely to be buried soils containing cultural material several thousand years old and numerous shallow disturbances associated with the World War I barracks and the more recent firing ranges that once occupied the site.

Rather than pick away at the surface to little effect, given the size of the site and the potential depths of cultural material, we decided to excavate a number of backhoe trenches. The goal was to expose the stratification sequence and determine whether any of these strata contained cultural material. This would inform the main testing, to be done with an eight-inch power auger that could probe more than ten meters into the ground if necessary. Given the size of the area to be explored, we did not mind that several areas approximately 4 × 2 meters each were going to be destroyed by the backhoe, perhaps disturbing cultural material. It was a risk worth taking, because it would give us a very good idea of where we should conduct our less destructive tests.

As it turned out, the backhoe trenches exposed three different buried components across the project area, ranging from a near surface component of the Central Plains tradition (surface to about fifty centimeters), to Middle to Late Woodland (one-meter deep), to Late Archaic (two-meter deep) occupations below that. We were then able to conduct auger testing much more carefully and effectively than we could have without the trenching.

You may need to use heavy equipment for other reasons as well as when you must remove overburden quickly because of time constraints (i.e., a construction crew's bulldozers are idling in the background). Mechanical stripping, using a backhoe, road patrol, or belly scraper, may expose artifact concentrations or features very quickly but at the risk of damaging portions of features and artifact scatters.

Data recovery via hand excavation is obviously a better strategy if your goals are to record material in three dimensions so you can learn more about time and space relationships. The most efficient method is shovel skimming (a.k.a. shovel scraping or shovel shining), which is removal of soil with a very sharp shovel held at an acute angle to shave off a portion of the surface. An adept shoveler can remove earth in such fine levels that very little will be missed. If you risk disturbing delicate remains or missing smaller artifacts, it is best to trowel by hand.

The choice of technique depends in part on what you expect to find and what you intend to record. Clearly, there is a difference between excavating an artifact scatter and a hearth or other intact feature. In the former case, a shovel may suffice; in the latter, very light troweling and brushing are in order.

## DRY SCREENING

Whatever method you use, you always miss some artifacts, so the next step is usually screening of the soils you remove. Sifting excavated soils through a quarter- or eighth-inch screen is so simple when you are sitting in your office using your field school knowledge to create regulations for working archaeologists and so miserable when you are standing at a screen trying to break up hard lumps of earth or push damp clay through the mesh. It was a sly and cynical wag, no doubt, who gave the name "Love Slave" to one of the USD shaker screens. Screening, however, is a necessary task, because most data recovery techniques—except brushing, perhaps—miss some of the artifacts.

Carmichael and Franklin (1999) conducted a screen loss experiment at the KT site in New Mexico. Their results showed that quarter-inch screens may capture as little as 5 percent of lithic artifacts and miss many diagnostics, such as notching flakes, biface thinning flakes, initial edging flakes, and exotic raw materials. Surprised? USD archaeologists made a rather rare find in the region, a piece of obsidian from a sixty-mile highway corridor along the Floyd River in northwestern Iowa; the piece, recovered during the mechanical grade sorting of 10 percent sample bags of earth from excavation units at site 13PM407, was a piece of microdebitage of grade 5 (0.0469 inch, or 1.18 millimeters) (Molyneaux et al. 1996). The implications of the find were rather monumental in their simplicity: This chance excavation of a tiny part of a site along a large highway corridor yielded an artifact that someone chipped from a tool of material that originated far from this knoll along the Floyd River. Without screening we would never have been able to add to our knowledge of obsidian distribution and use in the region.

Basic screen design has not changed for generations. The most common form is the wooden box with a hardware cloth mesh, suspended from a tripod for long-term excavations or mounted on two legs with two handles for field surveys and short-term excavations. There are debates about which types are the most useful and easiest to use. If you work in an urban setting on large excavations and have dry earth to screen, you might consider a mechanical unit. A Gilson grade sorter with five screens will quickly reduce a pail of dirt to neatly sorted material and a tray of dust at the bottom. You might also search the websites of the industrial screening companies for innovative ideas. There are new mesh designs that work better with damp soils than the traditional square pattern; perhaps these would improve those long messy days of struggling with clay.

## WATER SCREENING AND FLOTATION

Water screening is the best method for ensuring more complete recovery of cultural material, as you literally wash away the soil. It is an especially good way to retrieve small artifacts and to track artifact loss through dry screening.

A number of different water screen set-ups are in use. The most primitive method combines a high-pressure pump, a hose, and ordinary box screens. Self-contained sluice boxes and barrel systems (steel drums, fifty-five U.S. gallons or forty-five imperial gallons) pump water internally to stir up the soil. The barrel types may also double as flotation units if the light fraction can run off into a set of sieves. Do not assume that water screening makes life simple. Clay will sit in the screen unless it is physically disturbed. Pumps can be finicky. You will get wet and muddy. And you might find that there are regulations preventing the discharge of your soil back into the water.

Flotation is simpler, but don't misunderstand: If done properly it can also be very complex. You can buy or jury-rig a plastic bucket system with an inlet at the bottom and a spout at the top that draws off the waterborne fraction into a stack of sieves, or you can just fill a pail with water, dump the dirt in, stir it around, and scoop up the material with an ordinary kitchen sieve. Another approach is to pour it into a fine-mesh screen or cheesecloth. (See Toolkit, volume 5, for details on fine-screen recovery and processing methods.)

These are wonderful methods if you have carefully thought out why you are using them. If you retrieve a lot of light or heavy fraction, you may be facing long hours at a binocular microscope carefully separating the artifacts from the debris. Make sure these data will be useful. There is no point collecting seeds and other plant material unless you can differentiate between material associated with the site occupation(s) and modern material; there is equally no point in collecting microdebitage if you are only adding the numbers to your inventory. Are you going to use microdebitage to test your recovery methods? Do you think that the presence of microdebitage might indicate the precise spot that a knapper worked or reveal areas where larger pieces of debitage are absent because tool renovation (e.g., sharpening) rather than production took place there? You would miss such potentially significant data using conventional recovery methods.

## CONCLUSION

Collection strategies require careful planning, derived from the key questions in your research design. Failure to do effective planning can overwhelm you with useless data or cause you to miss important data. The truth is that most of us don't think that carefully about our approaches to data recovery and come to regret it once we get to the lab. We need to be more deliberate in our approaches to use our time, money, and other resources effectively.

A final element in data collection, discussed in chapter 6, relates to a variety of specialized types of data collection, ranging from samples for dating to human remains.

## 6

# RECOVERY OF SPECIALIZED MATERIALS AND SAMPLES

Specialized samples can and often should be taken to assist in the interpretation of sites and cultures. These samples often require specialized handling and extraction procedures. New techniques are being developed all the time, and the techniques discussed here are only some of those available. We note details of the collection procedures most relevant to interpretation of results. In the case of human remains, we focus on details that have a bearing on the eventual disposition of the remains. Specialized analytical techniques are continually undergoing refinement. Some researchers might argue it is inappropriate for archaeologists to charge our clients for the development of these advanced techniques, especially if they are still experimental and we can't yet be sure how to interpret the results. To the contrary, we believe that archaeologists must continue to try new techniques in the context of CRM excavation. Most archaeological sites excavated in the United States today are studied because they are determined eligible for the National Register of Historic Places for their information potential. A stratified lithic scatter may not inform us about the beginnings of agriculture, or ceramic production areas, but if the lithics are obsidian, the site may have considerable research potential either because it can help establish a regional hydration chronology or because it can be analyzed in the context of an existing chronology. We will never work the bugs out of new technologies if we do not apply them on real archaeological sites, and we won't be giving our clients our best efforts if we do not address the real research potential of the sites we are privileged to excavate.

## CHRONOMETRIC SAMPLES

Numerous methods can be used to date deposits or artifacts. Some of these methods are easier and less expensive to use than others, but in all cases, it is good to run multiple samples. More is better, as this helps you decide which dates may be aberrant. We like to run at least ten dates from a site, and it really helps to have some of the samples ordered by stratigraphy, so the span of occupation can be dated and aberrant dates can be identified. When possible, it is also a good idea to use multiple dating techniques. Dendrochronology and radiocarbon are the oldest of these methods, and most of the other methods are interpreted by making correlations with these two.

## DENDROCHRONOLOGY

Tree ring dating was developed in the early twentieth century in the Southwest, where many of the ruins contained large logs as structural support beams. A. E. Douglass (1936) observed that the widths of rings in the logs varied and that sequences of rings appeared to have patterns representing wet and dry years. He began collecting samples from living trees and archaeological sites to build a master chart from overlapping rings. By 1936, his chronology extended back to A.D. 700.

Subsequent work has developed chronologies of a millennium or more in many regions of the United States and Latin America. Dendrochronology has dated hundreds of archaeological sites and has provided the key to calibrating radiocarbon ages to calendar years. Dendrochronology also is revealing major shifts in global and regional climate patterns. Collection of old wood samples for dendrochronology is important for understanding changes in local adaptations as well as more general processes of climate–culture relationships. From this perspective, well-preserved dead trees are significant historic resources.

Dendrochronology is becoming a major method of dating log structures in the East. On historic sites and old farms, it can reveal much about landscape evolution. Projects that remove trees, such as reservoirs and highways, should have dendrochronology samples taken from the largest and most stressed trees (those whose growth is most significantly affected by annual or seasonal weather changes). Waterlogged, preserved trees in swamps should be extensively sampled.

When taking samples, it is best to consult with a specialist, as there are various ways to collect samples, depending on the allowable impact to the sampled tree or log. If trees are being cut, take the sample from about a foot above the ground. Cut the stump horizontally and then make two five- to six-centimeter-deep parallel cuts about five centimeters apart, with the center of the tree in the middle. Cut the section off, and label the provenience of the sample. Contextual data should include natural context (e.g., yard, fenceline, virgin forest, etc.), species, and map coordinates. Samples from log cabins that are being destroyed or are in an advanced state of decay may be similarly taken and also should be labeled by wall and log number.

If the tree, cabin, or pueblo will be preserved, take samples with an increment borer that removes a one-centimeter-diameter core. The living tree can heal over the wound in a year or two, but it is important to cover it with grafting tar. To get close to a true cutting date when sampling structural logs, try to take the core so that exterior rings are included. Whether or not exterior rings are included should be noted on the label. The samples may be bagged or boxed in cardboard or paper and allowed to air dry slowly.

Charred archaeological sections need to be supported, undercut, and wrapped in aluminum foil and carefully bagged in polyethylene. Samples should be carefully air dried. Waterlogged specimens need special treatment. Contact an experienced specialist whenever working on wet sites.

## RADIOCARBON SAMPLES AND DATES

Radiocarbon dating is a standard method that can be applied to virtually any once-living organism (see Toolkit, volume 4, for background). Radiocarbon samples should be taken whenever suitable carbon or other organic material is observed in the excavations. These samples should be assigned unique field serial numbers (FSNs) and their locations should be plotted on plans and profiles.

Take samples with a clean trowel, forceps, or other small excavating tool. Samples should be handled as little as possible, and they should not be directly touched at all, as the oils from the excavator's hands can contaminate the sample, yielding a spurious young date. For the same reason, smoking materials should not be permitted within or near the excavation units lest they blow into an area where a radiocarbon sample is being collected. Place the sample in an aluminum foil pouch and close up the pouch. Label the sample with provenience, FSN, date, and initials and place it in a plastic bag. Note the nature of the contents, such as wood charcoal, corn kernel, leaf, or nut hull.

Standard samples should have ten grams of carbon for normal counting, which costs about $250 per sample. Accelerator mass spectrometry dates samples as small as a fraction of a gram, but analysis costs about twice as much. High precision dating of seeds from annual plants greatly increases the probability that the date is accurate for the targeted event, stratum, or feature. Scattered wood carbon is not a preferred sample type but is better than nothing. Scattered wood may derive from the interior of one or more trees or may derive from older tree falls or dead wood, which could date from hundreds of years prior to the target event, such as the burning of a building. Scattered flecks of wood charcoal often produce dates with very large standard deviations (± ranges) because they are made up of different-aged wood. On the other hand, dates on the external rings of logs or posts from structures can precisely date the erection of the building.

It is sometimes possible to identify the effects of old wood dates on archaeological sites by collecting and submitting multiple radiocarbon samples. The use of old wood may yield a pattern of radiocarbon dates in which some "unacceptably early" dates are followed by a cluster of later dates that probably estimate the actual time of occupation (Carmichael 1985:321–22). This pattern has been observed within individual features at several sites in the El Paso area, where dates for a single hearth feature span a range of seven hundred years, with a cluster of dates at the late end of the range (Hard 1983:56–57). When working in areas where the old wood problem is a potential concern, we highly recommend collecting a large number of quality samples and submitting multiple samples, even from the same feature. Your archaeobotanist should identify the species of the wood samples before they are submitted for dating. Avoiding samples from decay-resistant species and favoring short-lived species or annuals can reduce the likelihood of obtaining old wood dates. If all the collected samples are of resistant species, then at least you will be forewarned of the potential problem.

Sometimes it is advantageous to select radiocarbon samples from the analyzed flotation samples. Your archaeobotanist can select seeds or other charcoal whose direct may be important in understanding the site inhabitants' patterns of plant use. Obtain C13/C14 ratios in all dated samples to learn about their composition and to permit more accurate calibration to calendar years.

Upon completion of the fieldwork, there will likely be scores or hundreds of samples and enough money to run only a fraction of the total. Some samples will be of higher quality, and some will be from key features or stratigraphic profiles. When you can choose from among many samples, it is always good practice to run three or more dates that are in known, relative stratigraphic positions.

Dates should always be presented clearly in a table that shows the laboratory number, FSN, provenience, the lab date in radiocarbon years B.P., and the tree ring calibrated intercepts and range at the two sigma level. Use the most recent release of the standard calibration software (http://calib.org).

## ARCHAEOMAGNETIC DATING

Archaeomagnetic dating relies on the fact that the Earth's magnetic poles shift over time. When iron-rich soil is fired, the iron particles will align to the then-current orientation of the Earth's magnetic field. At times during the Holocene, magnetic north has been as far south as Hawaii. Dates are determined by knowing the past orientations to magnetic north from a particular locality. The magnetic shifts are documented by correlation with radiocarbon dates. The precision of the radiocarbon dates thus limits that of the archaeomagnetic dates; however, at a particular locality, the relative dates could have a relative precision to each other of about twenty-five years.

Before taking archaeomagnetic samples, take a short training workshop with one of the method's practitioners (see www.u.arizona .edu/~slengyel). Samples are taken from very well-burned, almost brick-hard, oxidized clay. Three one-centimeter cubes are excavated in situ and oriented to magnetic north. Brass molds are placed over the samples and plaster of paris is poured into the mold and allowed to dry. Magnetic north is precisely inscribed in the plaster. Getting magnetic north correct is very important. The blocks are undercut, bagged separately in polyethylene, and labeled with provenience, date, and collector. Archaeomagnetic samples are expensive to take; however, establishing master curves for a region can result in more precise dates.

## THERMOLUMINESCENCE (TL) DATING

TL dating is based on principles of quantum mechanics. When a substance is subjected to radiation, its electrons are "kicked" to higher orbits. When that material is heated the electrons return to their lower, less energetic state and give off a flash of visible light, which is measurable. To be datable, a sample must have been heated in the time period one is trying to date and then protected from further heating. Substances containing silica are good for dating purposes, particularly potsherds, fire-cracked sandstone, and heat-treated chert. The amount of radiation at the particular site also must be measured, so soil samples must be taken along with the samples to be dated, or the background radiation may be measured with a dosimeter.

TL dating has not been particularly popular because it costs about twice as much as standard radiocarbon dating, and results are not as reliable. However, TL does permit direct dating of artifacts and dating sites at which carbon is not preserved. (See sidebar 6.1 to read about how TL dating was used at one site.)

When taking TL samples, keep them cool. Bag in plastic or paper collection bags, and label the bags like other artifacts. Plot the location of the sample's FSN on appropriate plans and profiles. Don't place them in black plastic bags and leave them in the sun. As with radiocarbon dates, try to process at least three samples, preferably in stratigraphic relation to each other so it is possible to see whether they are consistent.

Use common sense in selecting samples that target the event, stratum, or feature you are trying to date. For example, with dating pottery, sherds with pristine breaks rather than eroded sherds are preferred because the eroded sherds are likely to have been kicked around the site for a long period of time before they were deposited into the archaeological record.

## OXIDIZABLE CARBON RATIO (OCR) DATING SAMPLES

OCR is a recently developed and controversial method of dating pedogenesis in aerobic soils. The method, developed by Douglas Frink (1994), is based on complex relations among the parameters of soil development and the recycling of carbon through the soil to living plants. OCR has been calibrated with radiocarbon dates and has a very high statistical correlation with other dates. The method dates

## 6.1.  TL DATING AT 3WA539

At 3WA539, we realized toward the end of the project that there was virtually no carbon to date, but there was a lot of fire-cracked rock and heat-treated chert. We contacted Dr. Ralph Rowlett at the University of Missouri, who was then running TL dates at very reasonable rates. To get the background radiation counts, his preference was to set dosimeters into the site for a month. Fortunately, the remaining portion of the site had not been bulldozed, and our baulks were intact. The other alternative would have been to take a cup of soil with each sample, and we did not have soil associated with each sample of fire-cracked rock. We did have a sample of two pieces of fire-cracked rock from each provenience in which it occurred. The bulk of the rock assemblage had been counted, weighed, and discarded because most repositories do not like to maintain such collections forever. However, it is always good to keep a sample of each category discarded because one never knows what new analytical methods will be developed in the future (see Toolkit, volume 6). We were happy that we had the fire-cracked rock samples from everywhere on the site.

At 3WA539, the TL dates showed that use and reuse of the large fire-cracked rock feature spanned the time from 3000 B.P. until about the year 1000. The dates suggest that at the beginning of the Mississippian period, an economic shift occurred, and this site dropped out of use. We know from other data that this was about when corn was introduced into the region.

the soil development; in the case of a pit feature or other archaeological deposit, this may or may not be the same as dating the cultural activity.

Samples should be from as thin a level as possible; one centimeter thick is ideal. Thicker samples work, but with reduced precision. The samples should be one hundred grams dry weight, about a cup. A 20 × 20 × 1–centimeter area is adequate. Soil samples should be dried out as soon as feasible to prevent mold from growing. General and specific provenience and contextual information must be supplied on the form available from the laboratory.

At the Helm site (3HS449), samples were taken in a column from each soil stratum. The results showed that the alluvial terrace began to be deposited by 6000 B.P. and that the upper thirty centimeters built up during the past thousand years. The dates were reasonable geomorphically and consistent with other data (see sidebar 6.2).

### 6.2.  OCR APPLICATION AT THE HELM SITE

During the excavation of burials at the Helm site, the upper part of the pits was difficult to see until we actually saw the skeleton or grave goods. When the 2 × 2 unit over Burial 8 was excavated, we thought there was a pit because we saw B Horizon soils in the midden zone. It was a very small amount of soil, and once below the midden, no variation was observable across the unit floor. The floor was systematically examined with a penetrometer, with negative results. The feature was partially excavated, but no pit wall could be found. There were a few carbon flecks, but no color or hardness differences indicating a pit wall, as is the case in almost all features I (R.H.L.) had ever seen or known of. Yet, when excavation reached almost seventy centimeters below the surface, another burial was encountered. Three OCR dates were run from the soil samples that we had reserved from the flotation samples from the burials. The dates were consistent with the dates of the stratigraphic column and indicated that the different colored soils were reserved separately and were carefully refilled into the pit. This inference was consistent with findings of other investigators, which showed planned ceremonial segregation of different colored soils in Caddoan mounds.

## OBSIDIAN HYDRATION

A fresh fracture in obsidian will adsorb water from the atmosphere and form a microscopic layer of hydration. During the hydration process, sodium, lithium, and magnesium are leached out of the glass while hydrogen diffuses inward. This causes a mechanical strain at the glass surface and results in a hydration rim that is measurable in thin section under a microscope. Since the formation of the hydration layer is a diffusion process, the thickness of the rim is a function of the length of time elapsed since the fracture. Assuming that an appropriate rate of hydration can be determined, the rim thickness can be converted into calendar years (Michels et al. 1983). The two primary variables that must be controlled in order to determine the hydration rate are the chemical composition of the obsidian and the temperature under which the hydration process has proceeded. Researchers are still investigating the best ways to control the key variables in the hydration process.

Source-specific hydration rates must be determined because obsidians from different sources hydrate at different rates even if they occur on the same site, under the same temperature conditions. Fortunately, physical-chemical sourcing techniques such as X-ray fluorescence (Shackley 1995) permit identification of the sources of many obsidian artifacts. Sourcing has the added benefit of revealing the distance over which obsidian was transported, either as raw material or in tool form. In addition, if obsidian artifacts at a site can be shown to belong to the same chemical source group, then variation of hydration rim thickness within the group can be used as a relative dating technique.

The real attraction of obsidian hydration is its ability to directly date artifacts and assigning a chronometric as opposed to relative date. See Miller (1996) for a detailed review of the current state of obsidian hydration dating, and contact one of the experimental labs in advance of your excavation if you wish to apply the method.

## SOIL SAMPLES

Soil samples are useful for many different purposes including some of the dating methods just noted. Often they are useful for unanticipated analyses. It is a good practice to retain a cup or two of soil from flotation samples before they are floated in case the opportunity for other kinds of analyses arises. Such samples have allowed TL dating, OCR dating, pollen analysis, particle size analysis, and phytolith analysis, which otherwise could not have been preformed. Archive these samples with the collections for future use. While two-cup samples might be able to accommodate all of the following analyses, in most cases it is better to take samples for particular purposes.

Various kinds of chemical analyses can be performed on soil samples. Useful analysis can be as simple as standard pH tests or as complex as trace element analysis performed with a mass spectrometer or nuclear reactor. Required sample sizes vary from very small to a cup for most analyses. Agricultural laboratories often can analyze soil chemistry for a nominal cost. What is appropriate is dependent on research questions and preservation. It is always better to take more samples than you expect to need because new questions and different ways of testing project hypotheses always present themselves, and sometimes these samples can provide answers.

## FLOTATION SAMPLES

Sampling for flotation is discussed in volume 5 of this series. Here are a few highlights to keep in mind during excavation.

Flotation samples are primarily intended to recover small, charred fragile plant and animal remains. When taking flotation samples, it is most desirable to cut out the whole sample with one or a few cuts or to chunk out the sample in pieces of manageable size. Thin-slicing the whole sample is not a good practice because it also slices the botanical remains. These remains are so fragile that rapidly changing moisture states can reduce them to unrecognizable dust. For short-term storage, store samples in polyethylene bags to help preserve their moisture stability or in sandbags for long-term storage. Lafferty, running his first project, was marveling at the great preservation of the charred walnut shell that was coming out of the flotation samples that were drying in the sun. He went to look at these half and three-quarter hulls about noon, and they were little piles of dust. Always dry samples as slowly as possible, and avoid rehydrating them once they are dry.

Label the outside of the sample bag with waterproof, rotproof tags (felt-tipped pen on flagging tape), and seal another tag inside a small plastic bag within the sample bag.

## PARTICLE SIZE/GEOMORPHIC SAMPLES

Samples for geological analysis are taken like other soil samples. They can help you identify geomorphic changes such as altered river flow and location, periods of loess deposition, or prehistoric earthquakes. Have your geologist take the samples or direct the sampling program. For fluvial histories, you must have cores or profiles from several parts of the terrace system and the swamps (see sidebar 6.3 for one example). Geomorphologists like to have backhoe trenches all the way across a valley, but this is seldom possible.

## POLLEN AND PHYTOLITH SAMPLES

Pollen samples from features and burials can document the use of plant materials not present in other parts of the deposits, and pollen

## 6.3.  THE PEMISCOT BAYOU CORE

The Pemiscot Bayou core was one of over twenty cores that were taken to give the Corps of Engineers some baseline data on the likely locations of buried sites between the Mississippi River and Big Lake. The core was also selected for dating and pollen analysis to form a dated pollen chronology for the region.

The Pemiscot Bayou core was taken near the Eaker site. It took most of a day to extract this core using a commercial coring rig mounted on a 2.5-ton truck. The core driver has five-foot-long segments of driving steel. Each time a meter of core is taken, the driving segments have to be disassembled and then reassembled to proceed to the next segment. The deeper the core goes, the longer this process takes. A geomorphologist described the different strata as the core was extracted and properly labeled each core segment. It took almost all day to take the 5.8-meter-long core.

The geomorphologist subsampled the strata for particle size analysis to study the depositional environments, extracted carbon to send for radiocarbon dating, and sent twenty-three samples of the core for pollen analysis (Scott and Aasen 1987).

There were twenty strata in the Pemiscot Bayou core, which included five buried paleosols. This analysis showed change in the geological environment of Pemiscot Bayou over more than eight thousand years. About eight thousand years ago, a large natural levee was at the core site that was probably adjacent to the main course of the Mississippi River (Guccione 1987). About 6,500 years ago, the core area became a large backwater swamp as the river avulsed or migrated to the east. Around the year 1000, Pemiscot Bayou incised itself and formed a natural levee and then a channel that filled in rather recently.

cores from anaerobic or dry deposits can document environmental changes. Pollen and phytolith sampling is addressed in volume 5 of the Archaeologist's Toolkit series.

It is always a good idea to take pollen cores adjacent to sites that are being extensively excavated because a dated core will give you a good idea of local vegetation and landscape evolution. Pollen sequences are preserved best in undisturbed lakebed, backwater, and wetland deposits.

## PROTEIN RESIDUE SAMPLES

Proteins may be preserved on stone tools for thousands of years (Loy 1983). Specialists can often determine the species of plants and animals processed by these tools. At 3WA741, we took samples and tested them for the presence of blood. While this was a rather simple test, using commercially available urine blood test "litmus" strips, it suggested that many of the ground stone artifacts usually assumed to have processed plants, such as metates and pitted cobbles, had blood protein on them (Lafferty et al. 1996). Subsequent work at another site in the Ozarks showed that rabbits were being processed with "nutting stones."

Stone tools to be sampled for protein residue should be identified in the field and not washed. They should be handled as little as possible, bagged in zip-lock bags, and labeled with appropriate provenience information. Add "DO NOT WASH" in large letters. Some investigators require excavators to use cotton curator gloves to avoid contamination.

## HUMAN REMAINS

Burials exist in many archaeological sites, and you often cannot predict their presence or absence. Sometimes the presence of burials may be reasonably inferred from the context (e.g., mounds), previous studies, diagnostic burial furniture, or feature shape. In some cases, testing will have revealed the presence of human remains. In one recent case, testing with a small backhoe encountered a burial. On that basis the site was determined to be significant. Excavation of the entire site, a Mississippian village, revealed that this was the only burial on the site, and it turned out to be the remains of a nineteenth-century African American male.

Clearly, human skeletal remains have considerable research potential. Just as clearly, all peoples have the right to be involved in determining how the remains of their ancestors are treated. The Native Americans Grave Protection and Repatriation Act (NAGPRA) requires agencies to consult with tribes regarding burials affiliated with the tribe or on tribal lands. Do consultation *before* excavation to assure that the tribe's feelings are known and respected. Come to agreement on such details as excavation methods, documentation, and packaging of the remains. Some tribes require that rites of purification be carried out under certain conditions. These matters need to be settled in advance, so allot the proper budget and schedule.

Many Native Americans consider bone preservatives, once commonly used to assist in the excavation of burials, inappropriate. In addition, care should be taken to ensure that all human remains are treated with proper respect during and following excavation. If you have any doubt about what constitutes proper respect, consult with the appropriate tribal groups prior to the initiation of excavation or at least prior to the excavation of any human remains.

An experienced bioarchaeologist or paleopathologist should direct the excavation of burials. Many observations can only be made when the burials are being excavated, and the literature is extensive and specialized.

## TOOLS

Excavation tools include those used in excavating features (appendix 1) as well as a specialized array for very fine work and to protect the bone from damage. Meticulous excavation is important. The field observations of bone imprints are often all that one finds from some burials. More commonly, human bone is poorly preserved. Bamboo or cane picks are good for working around bone. These can be easily shaped to different useful shapes, such as pointed or spatulated, and will not harm relatively solid bone. Dental picks are sometimes useful. Ask your dentist for his broken ones and reshape them. A set of small fine brushes is also essential. It is important to protect the excavations from the elements. Use either white or black shade cloth or tarps. Colored sunshades distort Munsell readings, and mixed colors make even consistent color observation impossible.

People react strongly when burials are exposed. In some areas of the country, the only reasonable thing to do is to hire guards so that someone is on the site twenty-four hours. If possible, keep a low profile with the press until the end of the project. (See sidebar 6.4. for the story of burials found at the Helm site.)

### 6.4.   HELM SITE BURIALS: PROBLEMS AND POTENTIALS

The Helm site (3HS449) was a small Caddo cemetery on the Ouachita River. The Arkansas Highway and Transportation Department (AHTD) had tested it and uncovered burial-shaped rectangular pits. Preliminary excavation in the pits had revealed intact Caddo pots. Caddo burial pots are smaller than their utilitarian

## 6.4. (Continued)

ware and were apparently produced solely as mortuary accompaniments. The AHTD placed twenty-four-hour armed guards on the site and began negotiating a memorandum of agreement with the Caddo Tribe of Oklahoma. The Caddo wanted no remains or associations packaged in plastic nor any photographs published. If bone was still preserved, they would perform the proper cleansing. The Caddo believe that when the bone has returned to the earth, the soul is released to return to the stars, and the burials are no longer sacred.

We began the excavation on the Helm site by hand excavating 2 × 2–meter units over the areas where the testing had indicated the cemetery lay. Flotation columns were taken from each unit. When each pit could be discerned, which was not easy, special treatment of the pit fills commenced. All excavated soil was returned to the laboratory for flotation processing. Beginning with the exposed bone, sometimes with only one exposed skeletal landmark, Dr. M. C. Hill could often tell where and about how large the burials were. The bone was dust, and the Caddo were kept informed daily (a cell phone was essential). They maintained that the ancestors had gone to the stars, and no Cedar Smoke Ceremony was required. We proceeded apace with strange windstorms, guards not showing up, and intruders being convinced to leave at gunpoint. At the end of the first week, a burial was encountered with the bone intact, and the Caddo said it was time for a Cedar Smoke Ceremony.

Once the burials were exposed, they were mapped. One burial had masses of red ochre in two places. Masses of small pebbles in another burial were probably rattles. Associations were mapped and assigned their own FSN, and pollen/flotation samples were removed from beneath the skull, each shoulder, midtorso, femora, tibiae, and ankles. The excavation revealed nine individuals in eight burial pits. The bone in most of the burials was so fragmentary that all that remained were stains and teeth. Seven of the burial pits contained two to four ceramic vessels. Analysis of the vessels by Ann Early suggested that three burials dated to the seventeenth- to eighteenth-century Deceiper phase and four burials from the fifteenth- to sixteenth-century Social Hill phase. This interpretation was consistent with the superposition and intrusions of several of the burials. The eighth burial, which contained no vessels, was intruded by a Social Hill and a Deceiper burial, suggesting that it was probably from the earlier Mid-Ouachita phase.

One burial from each phase was selected for analysis of pollen and phytolith samples, including samples from inside the ceramic vessels from each burial. The pollen analysis had some surprises. Linda S. Cummings reported that burials contained cotton (*Gossypium* sp.) pollen. The Hernando de Soto chroniclers mentioned that they saw cotton cloth in this region. Could this be confirming evidence, or had the pollen percolated down one meter at a later date? A half-liter soil sample from above burial 4 contained no cotton pollen. What was the source of the cotton pollen? We're not sure.

Honeysuckle (*Lonicera* sp.) pollen was identified in the midtorso area of both burials; perhaps the individuals ingested flowers for their sugar content, or flowers were placed on the bodies. Fern spores were recovered in the shoulder areas, suggesting either a cushion of fern fronds or possibly the use of fern stems in basketry. We know of no surviving Caddo baskets, but virtually all of the ethnographic accounts speak very highly of the skill of the Caddo basket makers.

When the last heavy flotation fraction was analyzed, the analyst asked Lafferty, "What about the nail that was in this sample?"

"Nail? What is that doing there?"

In a little zip-lock bag was a 21.3-millimeter-long piece of ferruginous metal. Its width tapered from 2.3 to 2.2 millimeters with a square cross-section. What was this, and how did it get there? We already knew that the site was around the right time to have been used when Hernando de Soto came through the region. Could this be the proverbial smoking gun?

We sent it along with two pieces of iron from the Martin Farm site in Florida, a known Soto site, to Dr. S. K. Nash at the University of Pennsylvania for metallurgical and elemental analyses of the three samples using particle-induced X-ray emission spectrometry and energy dispersive spectrometry. He concluded that because of its high manganese content, the Helm site specimen had to be a product of post-1860 technology. The location of the metal at the very bottom of a burial feature remains an enigma. Such a small piece might have fallen down a deep root hole; however, virtually no historic artifacts were on the surface, and the pollen distribution suggests that the burial was intact. It is also possible that sixteenth-century European military steel was more advanced than we think. Comparative analyses from that period are lacking.

Botanical materials were recovered and analyzed from the features, burials, and some of the overlying midden deposits. Analysis showed that the botanical remains in the grave fill were highly worn and eroded in secondary or even tertiary contexts. In composition they were similar to the midden.

## REBURIAL

It often comes as a surprise to archaeologists, but there is almost no subject on which all Native Americans agree. While there may be near-universal agreement that native groups should be involved in the determination of how the remains of their ancestors will be treated, the specifics of each case can vary widely. Sometimes basic skeletal research on the remains will be acceptable, and sometimes it won't. Sometimes nondestructive analyses will be acceptable, but destructive analyses won't. Sometimes even destructive techniques (such as radiocarbon dating or bone chemistry) may be approved. Sometimes reburial will be identified as the appropriate treatment, either before or after analysis, and either with or without the accompanying grave goods recovered in the excavation. Sometimes it will be permissible to retain a sample of the remains (such as tooth enamel) for future analysis, as long as the rest of the remains are reburied. Sooner or later, you will become involved in a project where human remains are reburied. By approaching the prospect with respect and sensitivity, it can be an informative and healing process, one that may be of considerable research value (see also sidebar 6.5).

### 6.5.  EXPERIENCES FROM THE REBURIAL ISSUE

A few years ago, one of us (D.L.C.) was called on by a Mescalero Apache holy man to assist him as an outside third party during consultations about the disposition of human remains discovered near the Mescalero reservation in New Mexico. When the question of research and reburial arose, I agreed that if he wanted the remains to be reburied, I would respect and support his wishes. He then asked what sorts of studies the archaeologists would like to do and what the possible benefits might be. I explained that standard anthropometric measurements and paleopathological observations could be made, but they would probably not teach us very much in this case. Given the state of research in the region, I suggested that it would be most useful to sacrifice some portion of the skeletal remains for radiocarbon dating and bone chemistry studies. After considering the destructive nature of these tests, the holy man agreed that they could proceed, as long as the rest of the remains were eventually reburied.

A few years earlier, we were both involved in the first reported reburial ceremony (figure 6.1) undertaken by a federal agency when the U.S. Air Force reburied the fragmentary remains of some twenty individuals recovered during archaeological testing at the Eaker site (3MS105) in northeastern Arkansas (Brown 1991). In this case, the human remains were analyzed as part of Section 106 compliance and determined to have no further research potential (Lafferty et al. 1989). Throughout the test excavations, the Air Force had consulted with the Quapaw tribe of Oklahoma, who claim descendancy from the site's occupants. Funds were provided to bring a tribal delegation from Oklahoma, including holy man Bob Whitebird and several members of the Quapaw tribal council. The Air Force halted air traffic at the base for more than an hour so the ceremony could be undertaken with hushed reverence, a simple act of respect by a federal agency that spoke volumes to people who were directly affected by our excavations.

Following the reburial ceremony, at an impromptu ethnographic interview, Bob Whitebird spoke of his people and their past. The occasion and the emotion of the moment elicited a traditional story that had never been heard by the tribal council members. So, in response to diverse interests and constituencies, a major archaeological site was preserved, human remains were studied and reburied, and archaeologists, leaders of the Quapaw tribe, and U.S. Air Force personnel consulted and cooperated in a spirit of respect. In the end, the archaeological project at Eaker Air Force Base also contributed to a fuller understanding of the Quapaw people. How satisfying for everyone concerned; how appropriate for archaeology to be anthropology.

Figure 6.1.    Repatriation ceremony at Eaker Air Force Base, conducted by Quapaw holy man Bob Whitebird. (Photograph by Sergeant Christine Richards.)

## LOOKING TO THE FUTURE

As with other data recovery methods and techniques, collection of specialized samples has grown more complex as technologies have developed. For archaeologists whose careers span a few decades, the rapidly changing technologies sometimes seem amazing and a bit overwhelming because they allow us to develop data types for which we might not have dared hope at the beginning of our careers. Predictive models have increased in sensitivity, assisted by computers and GIS, allowing us to locate sites with somewhat greater reliability than our intuition and experience. Remote sensing has granted us something close to X-ray vision so that we don't always have to dig, or at least so we can place excavations more effectively. New chronometric techniques let us pry dates from materials and sample sizes we didn't imagine to be possible. Analytical techniques with environmental data have expanded our assessment of the interaction of the people of the past with their environments. It costs real dollars to collect and analyze specimens, and the increasing specialization among archaeologists has fostered fragmentation in our discipline. To be truthful, we have sometimes been incautious in our borrowing of new technologies. At the same time, whatever problems new technologies might bring, few among us would like to return to archaeology as it was practiced even a decade ago.

Changes in data recovery have also brought changes in our obligations to our publics. We need to be certain that we spend the public's money wisely as we apply these new technologies and not get carried away by our enthusiasms by thinking that these new approaches get us all that much closer to the "truth" about the past. They just provide us with more information which we still have to interpret. What we come up with can have an impact on the lives of contemporary people, and that is a responsibility of which we constantly must remain aware. All in all, however, we have a right to be excited for what will come in terms of new ways of knowing the archaeological past.

# APPENDIX 1

# EQUIPMENT, SUPPLIES, AND SOURCES FOR SPECIALIZED ANALYSIS

## PERSONAL TOOLKITS

1 Marshalltown pointing trowel (4.5-inch)
2 3-meter tape measures graduated in millimeters
1 line level
2 pins (gutter spikes, ten- to twelve-inch spikes, or surveyor pins)
1 notebook
2–3 meters of nylon staging twine
1 compass
1 fifteen- to twenty-centimeter ruler
Leather work gloves
Pencils

These are the basic tools that everyone should have in his personal tool kit. Most are available at your local hardware store or camping goods store. Marshalltown trowels have good welds—other brands of trowels will last as little as minutes on a site. Don't waste your money on other brands. Sharpen the leading edges to razor-sharp. Metric measuring tapes are often not carried in American hardware stores. Some tapes that are labeled as metric (e.g., three-meter tape) do not necessarily have metric graduations. Check the actual tape before you buy it. Various kinds of pins, such as wire spikes, gutter spikes, and surveyors pins, are useful in pulling line levels to check the depth of excavation levels and drawing profiles. Get a fluid-filled compass. They are faster.

## OTHER USEFUL TOOLS

Short-handled hoe
Ingalls pick
Ice cream scoop
Stainless steel tablespoon
Bamboo "Perino" pick
Clipboard
Whisk broom
Paintbrushes
Hand pruning shears

A short handled hoe is useful to level floors and clean profiles. Old hoes that are worn to one- to two-inch blade heights work best and often have better steel. Sharpen the side of the blade that faces the handle. Ingalls picks are useful in cleaning foundations, masonry, and around rocks. Ice cream scoops and various-sized scoops are useful in feature excavations. The Perino pick made of a wall of a large (2.5- to 5-centimeter diameter) bamboo is useful in working around fragile specimens and bone. (It is named after its inventor, the veteran excavator Greg Perino.) Sharpen one end to about a one-centimeter-wide bevel edge and the other to a point. Whisk brooms and various-sized paintbrushes are useful for cleaning excavation units, bringing out contrasting soil textures and so forth. Hand pruning shears are necessary to cut roots in forested environments.

## "COMPANY"-FURNISHED EXCAVATION EQUIPMENT

Here is a list of basic excavation equipment. This does not include the many expendable supplies, such as pencils, flagging, bags, and so forth, that are necessary. It also does not include equipment that might be required to excavate in caves, such as respirators, lighting, and hard hats, or in particularly deep units, like shoring.

Shovels
Picks/mattocks
Post hole digger
Coring equipment
Probes
Screens

Scoops
Dust pans
Hundred-meter tape measures
Plumb bob
Plane/drawing table
Field desk
Cameras
Mapping/surveying equipment
Munsell soil color charts
Hammers
First aid kit
Five- to ten-gallon water jug(s)
Dust masks in dry environments
OSHA manual
Scissors
Three-hole punch

Shovels come in a variety of shaped edges that are differentially useful in different situations. Flat shovels are most useful because we dig square holes, but other shapes are useful under different circumstances. Round-tipped shovels are good when one is excavating stones, and "sharpshooters" are indispensable when excavating clays. Shovels should be sharpened daily and cleaned and oiled after a project.

Picks/mattocks are important tools when working with rocky or very dry soils.

Post hole diggers are necessary to determine whether there are archeological deposits buried deeper than the intended excavation. Always keep a set handy.

Screens are very important and commercially available. Unfortunately, most that we have seen are based on the two-legged Roberts screen. They are hard to use and really hurt the back. Lafferty likes aluminum screens that are hung on a tubular aluminum A-frame. This arrangement is portable enough for testing projects.

## FORMS

Use forms to keep track of excavations data and to assure that the same type of information is recorded consistently. Forms may be created on your computer and copied. If you need thousands of copies, take them to a printer. Forms should be printed on acid-free paper. Excavation, feature, and burial forms should have green metric grid paper on the reverse. Forms generally include the following:

Field serial log or bag log
Photography log
Feature log
Excavation level form
Feature form
Burial form
Inside and outside bag tags

## EXPENDABLE SUPPLIES

Expendable supplies are necessary to support excavations. It is important to get these before the fieldwork, and get them in sufficient quantities to do the job. Commonly required expendable supplies include the following:

Stakes and pins
String/twine
Flagging tape
Pencils
Disposable water cups
Waterproof marking pens (Sharpies)
Masking tape
Duct tape
Three-ring binders for completed forms
Paper clips

## SOURCES OF TOOLS AND SPECIALIZED ANALYSES

The listing of a supplier or source here is not to be read as an endorsement of its services or products. Additional excellent vendors may be available.

## FIELD AND SURVEYING EQUIPMENT

Ben Meadows Co.
P.O. Box 5277
Janesville, Wisconsin 53547-5277
(800) 241-6401
www.benmeadows.com

Forestry Suppliers, Inc.
P.O. Box 8397
Jackson, Mississippi 39284-8397
(800) 360-7788
www.forestry-suppliers.com

## PLASTIC BAGS

Consolidated Plastics Company, Inc.
8181 Darrow Road
Twinsburg, Ohio 44087
(800) 362-1000
www.consolidatedplastics.com

Associated Bag Co.
400 W. Boden Street
Milwaukee, Wisconsin 53207
(800) 926-6100
www.associatedbag.com

Have good prices on all sizes and gauges of zip-lock bags.

## ARCHIVAL SUPPLIES AND EQUIPMENT

University Products, Inc.
517 Main Street, P.O. Box 101
Holyoke, Massachusetts 01041-101
(800) 628-1912
www.universityproducts.com

## RADIOCARBON DATING

Beta Analytic, Inc.
4985 SW 74 Court
Miami, Florida 33155
(305) 667-5167
www.radiocarbon.com

Beta offers standard and AMS dating with results in twenty to thirty business days. There are many other laboratories. If the dates are not calibrated, use the most recent calibration software available at http://calib.org.

## ETHNOBOTANICAL ANALYSIS

A number of individuals and organizations do this kind of analysis. Most of the larger anthropology departments have one or more ethnobotanists on the staff. Most investigators have several months' backlog. It is best to find someone who is familiar with the flora in your region. One active lab:

Paleo Research Institute
2675 Youngfield Street
Golden, Colorado 80401
(303) 277-9848

## DNA ANALYSIS

Paleoscience, Inc.
4989 SW 74th Court
Miami, Florida 33155
(305) 662-7760
info@paleoscience.com

## ARCHEOMAGNETIC DATING

Dr. Jeff Cox
Museum of New Mexico
P.O. Box 2087
Santa Fe, New Mexico 87504
(505) 827-6343
Also see www.u.arizona.edu/~slengyel

## DENDROCHRONOLOGY

Several laboratories work in different parts of the world. For a comprehensive list with interactive links, see the Ultimate Tree Ring Web Page at http://web.utk.edu/~Grissino/

## THERMOLUMINESCENCE DATING

Dr. James Feathers
Department of Anthropology
Box 353100
University of Washington
Seattle, Washington 98195-3100
(206) 685-1659
jimp@u.washington.edu

## OXIDIZABLE CARBON RATIO DATING

Dr. Douglas S. Frink
Archeological Consulting Team, Inc.
P.O. Box 145
Essex Junction, Vermont 05453-0145
(802) 879-2017
dsfrink@aol.com

# APPENDIX 2

# CONVERSION TABLES AND OTHER USEFUL RESOURCES

Basic trigonometry and geometry are necessary to lay out square units and often in site grid layout. The most important is the relationship of the hypotenuse of the right triangle. The Pythagorean theorem tells us that the square of the hypotenuse is equal to the sum of the squares of the other two sides (legs). Expressed mathematically where $A$ and $B$ are the legs of a right triangle and $C$ is the hypotenuse, this is:

For a $1 \times 1$ unit:

$$C^2 = A^2 + B^2 = 1(1) + 1(1)$$
$$C^2 = 1 + 1$$
$$C^2 = 2$$
$$C = \text{square root of } 2$$
$$C = 1.4142135$$

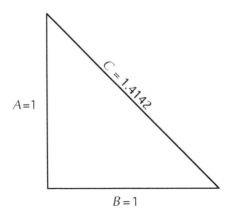

This ratio is worth memorizing as one is always using it to set up square units, extend the grid, or calculate how high a bluff is. Because we always use square units, this is a linear relationship. If one needs to pull in a 10 × 10–meter block, then pull the 10-meter leg out from the grid and pull the 14.1421-meter hypotenuse to set the new point (see tables A2.1 and A2.2).

**Table A2.1.  Hypotenuses of different-sized units**

| Unit Size | Hypotenuse |
|---|---|
| 1 × 1 | 1.4142 |
| 2 × 2 | 2.8284 |
| 3 × 3 | 4.2426 |
| 5 × 5 | 7.0711 |
| 10 × 10 | 14.1421 |
| 100 × 100 | 141.4213 |

**Table A2.2.  Conversion factors**

| Multiply | By | To obtain |
|---|---|---|
| Acres | 43,560 | Square feet |
| Acres | 0.4047 | Hectares |
| Acres | 4,047 | Square meters |
| Acres | $1.562 \times 10^{-3}$ | Square miles |
| Acre feet | 43,560 | Cubic feet |
| Board feet | 144 sq. in. × 1 in. | Cubic inches |
| Bushels | 1.244 | Cubic feet |
| Bushels | 2,150 | Cubic inches |
| Bushels | 0.03524 | Cubic meters |
| Bushels | 4 | Pecks |
| Bushels | 64 | Pints (dry) |
| Bushels | 32 | Quarts (dry) |
| Centimeters | 0.3937 | Inches |
| Centimeters | 0.01 | Meters |
| Centimeters | 10 | Millimeters |
| Chains | 66 | Feet |
| Chains | 100 | Links |
| Chains | 0.0125 | Miles |
| Cubic centimeters | $6.102 \times 10^{-2}$ | Cubic inches |
| Cubic centimeters | $10^{-6}$ | Cubic meters |
| Cubic centimeters | $2.642 \times 10^{-4}$ | Gallons |
| Cubic centimeters | $10^{-3}$ | Liters |

**Table A2.2.  Conversion factors (*continued*)**

| Multiply | By | To obtain |
|---|---|---|
| Cubic feet | 0.02832 | Cubic meters |
| Cubic feet | 0.03704 | Cubic yards |
| Cubic feet | 7.481 | Gallons |
| Cubic feet | 28.32 | Liters |
| Cubic inches | 16.39 | Cubic centimeters |
| Cubic inches | $5.787 \times 10^{-4}$ | Cubic feet |
| Cubic inches | $1.639 \times 10^{-5}$ | Cubic meters |
| Cubic inches | $2.143 \times 10^{-5}$ | Cubic yards |
| Cubic inches | $4.329 \times 10^{-3}$ | Gallons |
| Cubic inches | $1.639 \times 10^{-2}$ | Liters |
| Cubic meters | $10^6$ | Cubic centimeters |
| Cubic meters | 35.31 | Cubic feet |
| Cubic meters | 1.308 | Cubic yards |
| Cubic meters | $10^3$ | Liters |
| Cubic yards | 27 | Cubic feet |
| Cubic yards | 0.7646 | Cubic meters |
| Cubic yards | 202.0 | Gallons |
| Fathoms | 6 | Feet |
| Feet | 30.38 | Centimeters |
| Feet | 0.3048 | Meters |
| Feet | 0.36 | Varas |
| Furlongs | 40 | Rods |
| Gallons | 0.1337 | Cubic feet |
| Gallons | 231 | Cubic inches |
| Gallons | 3.785 | Liters |
| Gallons | $3.785 \times 10^{-3}$ | Cubic meters |
| Gallons | 8 | Pints (liquid) |
| Gallons | 4 | Quarts (liquid) |
| Gills | 0.1183 | Liters |
| Grains (troy) | 0.6480 | Grams |
| Grams | 0.03527 | Ounces |
| Hectares | 2.471 | Acres |
| Inches | 2.540 | Centimeters |
| Kilograms | $10^3$ | Grams |
| Kilograms | 2.2046 | Pounds |
| Kilograms | $1.102 \times 10^{-3}$ | Tons |
| Knots | 1.152 | Miles per hour |
| **Leagues** | | |
| English | 3.0 | Miles |
| Gallic | 2.2530 | Kilometers |
| Gallic | 1.4 | Mile |
| Gallic | 1.25 | Roman mile |
| French, common | 4.4481 | Kilometer |
| French, common | 2.764 | Mile |
| French, Post | 3.8977 | Kilometer |

**Table A2.2.   Conversion factors (*continued*)**

| Multiply | By | To obtain |
|---|---|---|
| **Leagues (continued)** | | |
| French, Post | 2.422 | Mile |
| Flemish | 6.2763 | Kilometer |
| Flemish | 3.9 | Mile |
| **Sixteenth-century Spanish** | | |
| League comun | 5.57 | Kilometers |
| League comun | 3.45 | Miles |
| League legal | 4.19 | Kilometers |
| League legal | 2.63 | Miles |
| Links (surveyor's) | 0.01 | Chains |
| Links (surveyor's) | 7.92 | Inches |
| Liters | $10^3$ | Cubic centimeters |
| Liters | 0.03531 | Cubic feet |
| Liters | 61.02 | Cubic inches |
| Liters | $10^{-3}$ | Cubic meters |
| Liters | $1.308 \times 10^{-3}$ | Cubic yards |
| Liters | 0.2642 | Gallons |
| Liters | 1.057 | Quarts |
| Meters | 100 | Centimeters |
| Meters | 3.2808 | Feet |
| Meters | 39.37 | Inches |
| Meters | $10^3$ | Kilometers |
| Meters | 1.0936 | Yards |
| Miles | 5280 | Feet |
| Miles | 1.6093 | Kilometers |
| Miles | 80 | Chains |
| Miles | 1900.8 | Varas |
| Ounces | 28.35 | Grams |
| Pounds | 453.6 | Grams |
| Rods | 16.5 | Feet |
| Square feet | $2.296 \times 10^{-5}$ | Acres |
| Square feet | 0.09290 | Square meters |
| Square inches | 6.425 | Square |
| centimeters | | |
| Square kilometers | 0.3861 | Square mile |
| Square meters | $2.471 \times 10^{-4}$ | Acres |
| Square meters | 10.764 | Square feet |
| Square miles | 640 | Acres |
| Square miles | 2.590 | Square kilometers |
| Square varas | 7.716049 | Square feet |
| Square varas | 0.857339 | Square yards |
| Square yards | 0.8361 | Square meters |
| Square yards | 9 | Square feet |
| Tons (metric) | $10^3$ | Kilograms |
| Tons (metric) | 2,205 | Pounds |
| Tons (long) | 2,240 | Pounds |

**Table A2.2.    Conversion factors (*continued*)**

| Multiply | By | To obtain |
|----------|-----|-----------|
| Tons (long) | 2,216 | Kilograms |
| Tons (short) | 2,000 | Pounds |
| Tons (short) | 907.2 | Kilograms |
| Varas | 2.7777 | Feet |
| Varas | 33.3333 | Inches |
| Varas | 0.9259 | Yards |
| Yards | 0.9144 | Meters |
| Yards | 1.08 | Varas |

Excerpted, by permission, from Eidenbach (1988).

## RANDOM NUMBER TABLES

Random numbers are useful for sampling of any kind and tables or generators are readily available on the web, in a range of books, and by using a software program such as Random Number Generator Pro at www.segobit.com/rng.htm (this is not an endorsement, but only an example) or even in Microsoft Excel. You can also find prepared tables online, print them, and take them to the field with you. On a web search engine, do a string search for "random number table," and you will find several as well as instructions on how to use them.

# REFERENCES

Adams, James L.
    1986   *Conceptual Blockbusting: A Guide to Better Ideas.* Addison Wesley, Reading, Mass.

Barker, Philip
    1983   *Techniques of Archaeological Excavation,* 2nd. ed., rev. and expanded. Universe: New York.

Binford, L. R.
    1962   Archeology as Anthropology. *American Antiquity* 28(2):217–25.
    1982   The Archaeology of Place. *Journal of Anthropological Archaeology* 1(1):531.

Brown, Judy
    1991   A Quapaw Reburial. *CRM* 14(5):24–27. National Park Service, Washington, D.C.

Carmichael, David L.
    1978   *Archaeological Assessment of the CHICAP Pipeline Easement.* Report prepared for Union Oil of California, through Nalco Environmental Services, Chicago. On file, Illinois Department of Conservation, Springfield.
    1985   *Archeological Excavations at Two Prehistoric Campsites near Keystone Dam, El Paso, Texas.* University Occasional Papers No. 14, New Mexico State University, Las Cruces, New Mexico.

Carmichael, David L., and Terry Franklin
    1999   Archeological Screening Techniques and Their Effects on the Recovery of Lithic Artifacts. In *Archaeology of the Jornada Mogollon: Proceedings from the 10th Jornada Mogollon Conference,* compiled by Michael Stowe and Mark Slaughter, pp. 151–56. GMI Press; Geomarine, Plano, Texas.

Claflin, W. H.
1931   *The Stalling's Island Mound, Columbia County, Georgia.* Papers of the Peabody Museum of American Archaeology and Ethnology, vol. 14, no. 1. Harvard University Press, Cambridge, Mass.

Cole, F. C., R. Bell, J. Bennett, J. Caldwell, N. Emerson, R. MacNeish, K. Orr, and R. Willis
1951   *Kincaid: A Prehistoric Illinois Metropolis.* University of Chicago Press, Chicago.

Davis, H. A. (ed.)
1982   *A State Plan for the Conservation of Archeological Resources in Arkansas.* Arkansas Archeological Survey Research Series 21, Fayetteville (Revised 1994).

Douglass, A. E.
1936   *Climatic Cycles and Tree-growth, Vol. III.* Carnegie Institution of Washington, Washington, D.C.

Dunnell, Robert C.
1984   The Ethics of Archaeological Significance Decisions. In *Ethics and Values in Archaeology,* edited by Ernestine Green, pp. 62–74. Free Press, New York.

Echo-Hawk, Roger C.
1993   Working Together—Exploring Ancient Worlds. *Society for American Archaeology Newsletter* 11(4):5–6.

Echo-Hawk, Walter R., and Roger C. Echo-Hawk
1991   Repatriation, Reburial, and Religious Rights. In *Handbook of American Indian Religious Freedom,* edited by Christopher Vecsey, pp. 63–80. Crossroads, New York.

Eidenbach, Peter L.
1988   *Archaeologists' Pocket Companion.* Human Systems Research, Inc. Tularosa, N.M.

Fagan, Brian M.
1985   *The Adventure of Archaeology.* National Geographic Society, Washington, D.C.

Figgins, J. D.
1927   The Antiquity of Man in America. *Natural History* 27(3):229–39.

Fowke, G.
1922   *Archeological Investigations.* Smithsonian Institution Bureau of American Ethnology Bulletin 76. Government Printing Office, Washington, D.C.

Fowler, Don D.
    1984   Ethics in Contract Archaeology. In *Ethics and Values in Archaeology*, edited by Ernestine Green, pp. 108–16. Free Press, New York.

Frink, D. S.
    1994   The Oxidizable Carbon Ratio (OCR): A Proposed Solution to Some Problems Encountered with Radiocarbon Data. *North American Archaeologist* 15:17–29.

Gifford, Carol A., and Elizabeth A. Morris
    1985   Digging for Credit: Early Archaeological Field Schools in the American Southwest. *American Antiquity* 50(2):395–413.

Guccione, M. J.
    1987   Geomorphology, Sedimentation, and Chronology of Alluvial Deposits, Northern Mississippi County, Arkansas. In Robert H. Lafferty III et al., *A Cultural Resources Survey, Testing, and Geomorphic Examination of Ditches 10, 12, and 29, Mississippi County, Arkansas*. Submitted to Memphis District, COE, Contract No. DACW66-86-C-0034 by MCRA Report No. 86-5, pp. 67–99.

Haas, Daniel
    1998   *The Federal Archeology Program, Secretary of the Interior's Report to Congress, 1994–95.* Archeology and Ethnography Program, National Park Service, U.S. Department of the Interior, Washington, D.C.

Haas, Jonathan
    1993   Discussant remarks delivered as part of the symposium, Two Years After: Repatriation and its Implementation. 58th Annual Meeting, Society for American Archaeology, April 17, St. Louis.

Hard, Robert J.
    1983   Excavation in the Castner Range Archaeological District in El Paso, Texas. El Paso Centennial Museum Publications in Anthropology, No. 11. University of Texas at El Paso.

Heizer, R. F.
    1959   *The Archaeologist at Work: A Sourcebook in Archaeological Method and Interpretation.* Harper, New York.

Hester, Thomas R., Harry J. Shafer, and Kenneth L. Feder
    1997   *Field Methods in Archaeology,* 7th ed. Mayfield, Mountain View, Calif.

Hill, A. T., and M. Kivett
    1949    Woodland-Like Manifestations in Nebraska. *Nebraska History*
            21(3):143–91.

Holmes, W. H.
    1903    Aboriginal Pottery of the Eastern United States. *Twentieth An-
            nual Report of the Bureau of American Ethnology to the Secre-
            tary of the Smithsonian Institution, 1898–99*, pp. 1–200.

Ives, John W. (ed.)
    1986    *Archaeology in Alberta, 1985.* Archaeological Survey of Alberta,
            Occasional Paper No. 29. Edmonton, Alberta.

Kellog, D. C.
    1987    Statistical relevance and site locational date. *American Antiq-
            uity* 52(1):143–150.

Kidder, A. V.
    1962    *An Introduction to the Study of Southwestern Archaeology.*
            Yale University Press, New Haven, Conn.

King, Thomas F.
    1977    Resolving a Conflict of Values in American Archaeology. In
            *Conservation Archaeology: A Guide for Cultural Resource
            Management Studies*, edited by Michael B. Schiffer and George
            J. Gummerman, pp. 87–96. Academic Press, New York.

King, Thomas F., and P. P. Hickman
    1973    *The Southern Santa Clara Valley, California: A General Plan
            for Archaeology.* A. E. Treganza Anthropology Museum, San
            Francisco.

Knudson, Ruthann, Francis P. McManamon, and Emlen Myers
    1995    *Report on the Federal Archeology Program (1988–1990).* U.S.
            Department of the Interior, National Park Service, Washington,
            D.C.

Lafferty, Robert H. III and Robert F. Cande
    1989    *Cultural Resources Investigations, Peacekeeper Rail Garrison
            Program, Eaker Air Force Base, Mississippi County, Arkansas.*
            Prepared for U.S. Air Force Regional Civil Engineer, AFRCE-
            BMS Norton Air Force Base, California by MCRA Report No.
            88-5.

Lafferty, Robert H. III, A. Early, M. C. Sierzchula, M. C. Hill, G. S. Powell,
N. Lopinot, L. S. Cummings, S. L. Scott, S. K. Nash, and T. K. Perttula
    2000    *Data Recovery at the Helm Site, 3HS449, Hot Springs County,
            Arkansas.* Submitted to Arkansas Highway and Transportation
            Department, Job FA3009. MCRA Report 2000-1.

Lafferty, Robert H. III, Margaret J. Guccione, Linda J. Scott, D. Kate Aasen, Beverly J. Watkins, Michael C. Sierzchula, and Paul F. Baumann
  1987  *A Cultural Resources Survey, Testing, and Geomorphic Examination of Ditches 10, 12, and 29, Mississippi County, Arkansas.* Submitted to Memphis District, COE, Contract No. DACW66-86-C-0034 by MCRA Report No. 86-5.

Lafferty, Robert H. III, N. H. Lopinot, M. J. Guccione, L. G. Santeford, Michael C. Sierzchula, S. L. Scott, K. A. King, K. M. Hess, and L. S. Cummings
  1988  *Tracks in Time,* National Park Service, Southwest Region Branch of CRM, Santa Fe, N.M.

Lafferty, Robert H. III, Lawrence G. Santeford, Margaret G. Guccione, Michael C. Sierzchula, Neal H. Lopinot, Kathryn A. King, Kathleen M. Hess, and Jody O. Holmes
  1987  *The Mitchell Site: 3WA58 Archeological Investigations at a Prehistoric Open-Field Site in Washington County, Arkansas.* Submitted to McClelland Consulting Engineers and the City of Fayetteville by MCRA Report No. 87-4.

Lafferty, Robert H. III, Lawrence G. Santeford, Michael C. Sierzchula, Robert F. Cande, Kathryn A. King, Carol S. Spears, and Robert A. Taylor
  1989  *A Corridor into Ozarkian Time: National Register of Historic Places Testing of 25 Sites in the AHTD Interstate 71 Corridor, Crawford and Washington Counties, AR.* Submitted to the Arkansas Highway and Transportation Department by MCRA Report No. 89-2.

Lafferty, Robert H. III, M. C. Sierzchula, R. F. Cande, P. B. Mires, M. T. Oates, M. J. Guccione, Neal Lopinot, L. G. Santeford, H. Wagner, S. Scott, and M. Cleaveland
  1996  *Cato Springs Archeology and Geomorphology: Archeological Data Recovery at 3WA539, 3WA577, and 3WA741, U.S. Highway Relocation, Washington County, Arkansas.* Submitted to Arkansas Highway and Transportation Department, Job 4833. MCRA Report 94-6.

Lafferty, Robert H. III, M. C. Sierzchula, G. Powell, N. Lopinot, C. Spears, and L. G. Santeford
  2002  *Data Recovery at the Hillhouse site (23MI699).* Report submitted to the Memphis District, Corps of Engineers, Contract DACW66-C-0032. MCRA Report 2001-1.

Layard, A. H.
  1849  *Nineveh and Its Remains.* John Murray, London.

Loy, Thomas H.
1989 Prehistoric blood residues: detection on tool surfaces and identification of species of origin. *Science* 220:1269–1271.

Lyman, R. Lee, Michael J. O'Brien, and Robert C. Dunnell
1997 *The Rise and Fall of Culture History.* Plenum, New York.

Lynott, Mark J., and Alison Wylie (eds.)
1995 *Ethics in American Archaeology: Challenges for the 1990s.* Society for American Archaeology. Allen, Lawrence, Kans.

Magne, Martin (issue editor)
1997 Parks Canada. *CRM* 20(4):3–62.

Meighan, Clement W.
1992a Some Scholars' Views on Reburial. *American Antiquity* 57(4):70410.
1992b University of California Give-Away of Museum Collections? *California Scholar* (Winter 1992–1993):23–25.
1993 The Burial of American Archaeology. *Academic Questions* 6(3):9–18.
1994 Burying American Archaeology. *Archaeology* 47(6):64–68.

Michels, J. W., I. S. T. Tsong, and G. A. Smith
1983 Experimentally Derived Hydration Rates in Obsidian Dating. *Archaeometry* 25(2):10–117.

Miller, Myles R. III
1989 *Archaeological Excavations at the Gobernadora and Ojasen Sites: Dona Ana Phase Settlement in the Western Hueco Bolson, El Paso County, Texas.* Center for Anthropological Research, Report No. 673. New Mexico State University, Las Cruces.
1996 The Chronometric and Relative Chronology Project, Section III: Obsidian Hydration Dating. Archaeological Technical Report No. 5. Prepared by the Anthropology Research Center, University of Texas at El Paso, for the Department of the Army, Directorate of the Environment, Fort Bliss, Texas.

Mills, William C.
1907 Explorations of the Edwin Harness Mound. *Ohio Archeological and Historical Quarterly* 16(2), Columbus.

Molyneaux, Brian L.
1983 The Study of Prehistoric Sacred Places: Evidence from Lower Manitou Narrows. Archaeology Paper No. 2. Royal Ontario Museum, Toronto.
2002 Exploring the Landscapes of Long-Distance Exchange: Evidence from Obsidian Cliffs and Devils Tower, Wyoming. In *Geochem-*

*ical Evidence for Long Distance Exchange,* edited by Michael Glascock, pp. 133–51. Bergin & Garvey, Westport, Conn.

Molyneaux, Brian L., Todd Kapler, Shesh Mathur, and Nancy J. Hodgson
    1993    A Phase II Survey of Segment I of the Highway Corridor. Prepared for RUST Environment and Infrastructure, Waterloo, Iowa.
    1996    Highway 60 Le Mars—Minnesota Border Archaeological Resources Survey.

Molyneaux, Brian L., William Ranney, Stephanie A. Spars, and Jason Kruse
    2002    Phase I and II Archaeological Reconnaissance and Testing on Alluvial Terraces at the Confluence of Threemile and Forsyth Creeks, Fort Riley, Kansas. Prepared for Dynamac Corporation, Fort Riley, Kan.

Morse, Dan F., and Phyllis A. Morse
    1983    *Archaeology of the Central Mississippi Valley.* Academic Press, New York.

Nelson, N. C.
    1916    Chronology of the Tano Ruins, New Mexico. *American Anthropologist* 18:159–80.

New Mexico State University (NMSU)
    1989    *Cultural Resources Report for the All American Pipeline Project, Santa Barbara, California to McCamey, Texas and Additional Areas to the East along the Central Pipeline Route in Texas.* Report submitted by All American Pipeline Company to the Bureau of Land Management, California Desert District.

Oakes, Yvonne R., and Dorothy Zamora
    1998    *Archaeology of the Mogollon Highlands: Settlement Systems and Their Adaptations.* Archaeology Note 232. Museum of New Mexico, Office of Archaeological Studies, Santa Fe.

O'Brien, Michael J.
    1996    *Paradigms of the Past: The Story of Missouri Archaeology.* University of Missouri Press, Columbia.

O'Laughlin, Thomas C.
    1980    *The Keystone Dam Site and Other Archaic and Formative Sites in Northwest El Paso, Texas.* Publications in Anthropology No. 8. El Paso Centennial Museum, University of Texas at El Paso.

Orton, Clive
    2000    *Sampling in Archaeology.* Cambridge University Press, Cambridge.

Parker, Patricia L., and Emogene Bevitt
    1997    Consultation with American Indian Sovereign Nations. *Common Ground: Archeology and Ethnography in the Public Interest* 2(3/4):22–27. National Park Service, Washington, D.C.

Patterson, L. W.
    1978    Basic Considerations in Contract Archaeology. *Man in the Northeast* 15–16:132–38.

Petrie, W. M. Flinders
    1901    *Diospolis Parva*. Egyptian Research Account, London.

Pitt Rivers, General
    1887–1898    *Excavations in Cranborne Chase, 1887–98*, vol. 4. Privately printed, London.

Plog, Fred
    1984    Ethics of Excavation: Site Selection. In *Ethics and Values in Archaeology*, edited by Ernestine L Green, pp. 89–96. Free Press, New York.

Pyburn, K. Anne, and Richard R. Wilk
    1995    Responsible Archaeology Is Applied Archaeology. In *Ethics in American Archaeology: Challenges for the 1990s*, edited by Mark J. Lynott and Alison Wylie, pp. 71–76. Society for American Archaeology, Allen, Lawrence, Kans.

Raab, L. Mark
    1984    Toward an Understanding of the Ethics and Values of Research Design in Archaeology. In *Ethics and Values in Archaeology*, edited by Ernestine Green, pp. 75–88. Free Press, New York.

Rapport, S., and H. Wright (eds.)
    1964    *Archaeology*. Washington Square Press, New York.

Rathje, William, and Cullen Murphy
    2001    *Rubbish!: The Archaeology of Garbage*. University of Arizona Press, Tucson.

Renfrew, Colin, and Paul Bahn
    1991    *Archaeology: Theories, Methods and Practice*. Thames & Hudson, London.

Rice, Glen E., and Fred Plog
    1983    A Formal Method for the Use of Backhoes in Archaeological Excavations. Manuscript on file, New Mexico State University.

Salazar, Virginia, and Jake Barrow (issue editors)
2000   Beyond Compliance: Tribes of the Southwest. *CRM* 23(9). US. Department of the Interior, National Park Service, Washington, D.C.

Scarborough, Vernon L.
1986   Meyers Pithouse Village: A Preliminary Assessment. In *Mogollon Variability*, edited by Charlotte Benson and Steadman Upham, pp. 271–84. University Museum Occasional Papers 15. New Mexico State University, Las Cruces.

Schiffer, Michael B., and George J. Gummerman (eds.)
1977   *Conservation Archaeology: A Guide for Cultural Resource Management Studies.* Academic Press, New York.

Scott, Linda J., and D. Kate Aasen
1987   Interpretation of Holocene Vegetation in Northeastern Arkansas. In Robert H. Lafferty III et al., *A Cultural Resources Survey, Testing, and Geomorphic Examination of Ditches 10, 12, and 29, Mississippi County, Arkansas.* Submitted to Memphis District, COE, Contract No. DACW66-86-C-0034 by MCRA Report No. 86-5, 133–150.

Shackley, M. Steven
1995   Sources of Archaeological Obsidian in the Greater American Southwest: An Update and Quantitative Analysis. *American Antiquity* 60(3):531–551.

Smith, Claire, and Heather Burke
2003   In the Spirit of the Code. In *Ethical Issues in Archaeology*, edited by Larry J. Zimmerman, Karen D. Vitelli, and Julie Hollowell-Zimmer, pp. 177–97. AltaMira, Walnut Creek, Calif.

Stapp, Darby C., and Michael S. Burney
2002   *Tribal Cultural Resource Management: The Full Circle to Stewardship.* AltaMira, Walnut Creek, Calif.

Stiger, Mark
1986   Proposal for the Archaic Phase Project at the Fillmore. Pass Site (FB-1613), Fort Bliss, Texas. Report on files, Directorate of Environment, Fort Bliss, Texas.

Swidler, Nina, Kurt E. Dongoske, Roger Anyon, and Alan S. Downer
1997   *Native Americans and Archaeologists: Stepping Stones to Common Ground.* AltaMira, Walnut Creek, Calif.

Tainter, Joseph A., and G. John Lucas
1983   Epistemology of the Significance Concept. *American Antiquity* 48:707–719.

Taylor, Jeanette
    1999    *River City: A History of Campbell River and the Discovery Islands.* Harbour, Madeira Park, British Columbia, Canada.

Taylor, W. W.
    1948    [1967] *A Study of Archeology.* Southern Illinois University Press, Carbondale.

Thomas, Cyrus
    1894    [1984] *Report on the Mound Explorations of the Bureau of Ethnology.* Smithsonian Institution, Washington, D.C.

Thomas, David Hurst
    1991    *Archaeology: Down to Earth.* Harcourt Brace Jovanovich College Publishers, Fort Worth, Tex.

Tylor, E. B.
    1871    [1958] *The Origins of Culture.* Harper & Row, New York.

Ucko, Peter J.
    1989    Foreword. In *Conflict in the Archaeology of Living Traditions,* edited by Robert Layton, pp. ix–xvii. Unwin Hyman, London.

Vogel, Gregory
    2002    *A Handbook of Soil Description for Archeologists.* Technical Paper No. 11. Arkansas Archeological Survey, Fayetteville.

Watkins, Joe, and Tom Parry
    1997    Archeology's First Steps in Moccasins. *Common Ground: Archeology and Ethnography in the Public Interest* 2(3/4): 46–51. National Park Service, Washington, D.C.

Wheeler, M.
    1954    *Archaelogy from the Earth.* Clarendon, Oxford.

Willey, Gordon R., and Jeremy A. Sabloff
    1993    *A History of American Archaeology,* 3d ed. Freeman, San Francisco.

Williams, Stephen
    2001    Reviewing Some Late 19th Century Archaeological Studies: Exploding the Myth of the "Myth." Paper presented at the Mid-South Conference, Memphis.

Wilson, Michael, Kathie L. Road, and Kenneth J. Hardy
    1981    *Megaliths to Medicine Wheels: Boulder Structures in Archaeology.* Proceedings of the Eleventh Annual Chacmool Conference,

Department of Archaeology, University of Calgary, Alberta, Canada.

Wormington, H. M.
1964   *Ancient Man in North America*, 5th ed. Denver Museum of Natural History Popular Series No. 4. Denver Museum of Natural History, Denver.

Zimmerman, Larry
1995   Regaining Our Nerve: Ethics, Values and the Transformation of Archaeology. In *Ethics in American Archaeology: Challenges for the 1990s*, edited by Mark J. Lynott and Alison Wylie, pp. 64–67. Society for American Archaeology, Allen Press, Lawrence, Kansas.

# INDEX

aboriginal vs. historic site, 9
academic archaeology, 3, 33–34
accelerator mass spectrometry, 76
accountability, 4, 10
AHTD. *See* Arkansas Highway and
  Transportation Department
American Anthropological
  Association, 47
American Museum of Natural
  History, 21
anthropology, archaeology as, 7–11
Apache site, 46–47, 88
archaeological excavation, as
  controlled destruction, 32;
  conservation ethic in, 41–42;
  justifying through research
  design/method, 6, 33, 39, 41,
  42–43; justifying through site
  selection/use, 33, 34–39, 35,
  36–38
archaeological excavation, use of, 2
archaeological research:
  academic/cultural resources
  management difference, 3, 33–34;
  constituent/consumer of, 28–29;
  cost of federally mandated, 4
Archaeological Resources Protection
  Act (ARPA), 5

archaeologist: ethical responsibility
  of, 6–7, 45–48; stereotype of, 29
archaeology: as anthropology, 7–11;
  definition of, 32; relevance of, 5
"Archaeology as Anthropology"
  (Binford), 27
archaeology theory, 26–28
archaeomagnetic dating, 77, 96
archival supplies/equipment, source
  for, 95
Arkansas Highway and
  Transportation Department
  (AHTD), 85, 86
ARPA. *See* Archaeological
  Resources Protection Act
auger testing, 12, 50, 51, 58, 69

backhoe trenching, 56–60, 57, 69
BAE. *See* Bureau of American
  Ethnology
Barker, Philip, 3
biface reduction technology,
  39–40
Binford, Lewis, 27
Bureau of American Ethnology
  (BAE), 21
Burial. *See* human remains
Burney, Michael S., 48

117

# ABOUT THE AUTHORS
# AND SERIES EDITORS

**David L. Carmichael** has twenty-eight years of experience in CRM archaeology and has been conducting applied ethnographic work with Native Americans for two decades. He has been involved in more than forty projects and has directed studies in twelve states throughout the West and Midwest. He received undergraduate training at the University of New Mexico and earned M.A. and Ph.D. degrees at the University of Illinois. He worked as a CRM contractor for sixteen years, served as the first tribal archaeologist for the Hopi Tribe, and authored the U.S. Air Force guidelines for consultation with Native Americans. His recent research has included the prehistoric archaeology of southern New Mexico and west Texas, Apache land use patterns, and Native American sacred sites. He teaches archaeology and anthropology at the University of Texas at El Paso.

**Robert H. Lafferty III** took his Ph.D. in 1977 from Southern Illinois University and is ROPA certified. He is a co-owner of Mid-Continental Research Associates, Inc. Since 1976, he has spent more than eighty-five months in the field directing all kinds of cultural resource management projects, and he has authored or principally coauthored fifteen books and more than a hundred smaller technical reports, articles, and papers. Many of his publications have centered on the chronology and cultural adaptation of prehistoric cultures in the Lower Mississippi Valley and the Ozark Mountains. During the past decade, he has been researching the chronology of prehistoric earthquakes in the New Madrid Seismic Zone with a team of geologists for the U.S. Geological Survey.

**Brian Leigh Molyneaux** is an archaeologist, writer, and photographer. He is a specialist in prehistoric art and society, the human use of the landscape, and computer-aided applications in archaeology. He is director of the University of South Dakota Archaeology Laboratory, codirector of the Missouri River Institute, and a research associate of the Royal Ontario Museum, Toronto. He received his M.A. in art and archaeology from Trent University, Peterborough, Ontario, in 1977 and his Ph.D. in archaeology at the University of Southampton, England, in 1991. His extensive fieldwork includes many years of travel in northern Canada, studying Algonkian rock art, ritual and religion, and archaeological research in the northern Great Plains. He recently conducted a two-year archaeological survey at Devils Tower National Monument, Wyoming. Dr. Molyneaux has published several books: *The Presented Past* (coedited with Peter Stone, Routledge, 1994), a study of archaeology, museums, and education around the world; *The Sacred Earth* (Little, Brown, 1995), a study of spirituality related to the landscape; *Native North America* (with Larry Zimmerman, Little, Brown, 1996), a detailed survey of Native North American culture, past and present; *The Cultural Life of Images* (editor and contributor, Routledge, 1997), a study of pictures and other visual representations of the past in archaeology; a new edition of *Native North America* (Oklahoma University Press, 2000); *Sacred Earth, Sacred Stones* (with Piers Vitebsky, Laurel Glen, 2001), a compilation dealing with spirituality in landscape and architecture; and *Mythology of the Americas* (with David M. Jones, Lorenz Books, 2001), a general encyclopedia. His rock art photographs have been exhibited in the National Gallery of Canada and featured in the PBS/BBC series, *Land of the Eagle*, and he is an active contributor to web-based symposia on art, technology, environment, and culture (e.g., The Anthology of Art, www.anthology-of-art.net, School of Fine Arts, Braunschweig, Germany).

**Larry J. Zimmerman** is the head of the Archaeology Department of the Minnesota Historical Society. He served as an adjunct professor of anthropology and visiting professor of American Indian and Native Studies at the University of Iowa from 1996 to 2002 and as chair of the American Indian and Native Studies Program from 1998 to 2001. He earned his Ph.D. in anthropology at the University of Kansas in 1976. Teaching at the University of South Dakota for twenty-two years, he left there in 1996 as Distinguished Regents Professor of Anthropology.

While in South Dakota, he developed a major CRM program and the University of South Dakota Archaeology Laboratory, where he is still a research associate. He was named the University of South Dakota Student Association Teacher of the Year in 1980, given the Burlington Northern Foundation Faculty Achievement Award for Outstanding Teaching in 1986, and granted the Burlington Northern Faculty Achievement Award for Research in 1990. He was selected by Sigma Xi, the Scientific Research Society, as a national lecturer from 1991 to 1993, and he served as executive secretary of the World Archaeological Congress from 1990 to 1994. He has published more than three hundred articles, CRM reports, and reviews and is the author, editor, or coeditor of fifteen books, including *Native North America* (with Brian Molyneaux, University of Oklahoma Press, 2000) and *Indians and Anthropologists: Vine Deloria, Jr., and the Critique of Anthropology* (with Tom Biolsi, University of Arizona Press, 1997). He has served as the editor of *Plains Anthropologist* and the *World Archaeological Bulletin* and as the associate editor of *American Antiquity*. He has done archaeology in the Great Plains of the United States and in Mexico, England, Venezuela, and Australia. He has also worked closely with a wide range of American Indian nations and groups.

**William Green** is the director of the Logan Museum of Anthropology and an adjunct professor of anthropology at Beloit College, Beloit, Wisconsin. He has been active in archaeology since 1970. Having grown up on the south side of Chicago, he attributes his interest in archaeology and anthropology to the allure of the exotic (i.e., rural) and a driving urge to learn the unwritten past, abetted by the opportunities available at the city's museums and universities. His first fieldwork was on the Mississippi River bluffs in western Illinois. Although he also worked in Israel and England, he returned to Illinois for several years of survey and excavation. His interests in settlement patterns, ceramics, and archaeobotany developed there. He received his master's degree from the University of Wisconsin at Madison and then served as Wisconsin SHPO staff archaeologist for eight years. After obtaining his Ph.D. from the University of Wisconsin at Madison in 1987, he served as state archaeologist of Iowa from 1988 to 2001, directing statewide research and service programs including burial site protection, geographic information, publications, contract services, public outreach, and curation. His main research interests focus on the development and spread of native agriculture. He has served as editor of the *Midcontinental Journal of Archaeology* and *The Wisconsin Archeologist*; has published articles in *American Antiquity*, *Journal of Archaeological Research*, and other journals; and has received grants and contracts from the National Science Foundation, National Park Service, Iowa Humanities Board, and many other agencies and organizations.